Left Behind

Nandini Murali is a diversity, equity and inclusion professional, and a certified life coach (with a focus on loss and transition). She has a doctorate in Gender Studies and is currently Vice-President, Learning & Research at Avtar, Chennai.

A suicide prevention and mental health activist, her lived experience of suicide loss inspired her to establish SPEAK (www.speakinitiative.org)—an initiative of MS Chellamuthu Trust and Research Foundation, Madurai, to create safe, supportive inclusive spaces to prevent suicide and promote mental health, SPEAK2us (93754 93754), a mental health helpline, and Project SPEAK, a postvention services initiative for women impacted by suicide loss, in collaboration with Mariwala Health Initiative, Mumbai.

A student of Vedanta, her daily spiritual practices enrich her personal space and her writerly life. Passionate about wildlife photography, Nandini loves to wander in forests with her camera. She is the author of six books that span genres as diverse as fiction, non-fiction, Indic Studies, translation and poetry. She can be contacted at nandini.murali8@gmail.com.

Left Behind

Surviving Suicide Loss

Nandini Murali

First published by Westland Publications Private Limited in 2021

Published by Westland Books, a divison of Nasadiya Technologies Private Limited, in 2023

No. 269/2B, First Floor, 'Irai Arul', Vimalraj Street, Nethaji Nagar, Alapakkam Main Road, Maduravoyal, Chennai 600095

Westland and the Westland logo are the trademarks of Nasadiya Technologies Private Limited, or its affiliates.

Copyright © Nandini Murali, 2021

Nandini Murali asserts the moral right to be identified as the author of this work.

ISBN: 9789357769853

10 9 8 7 6 5 4 3 2 1

The views and opinions expressed in this work are the author's own and the facts are as reported by them, and the publisher is in no way liable for the same.

Proceeds from the sale of this book will go to SPEAK, an initiative of MS Chellamuthu Trust and Research Foundation, Madurai.

All rights reserved

Typeset by Jojy Philip, New Delhi
Printed at Saurabh Printers Pvt. Ltd

No part of this book may be reproduced, or stored in a retrieval system, or transmitted in any form or by any means, electronic, mechanical, photocopying, recording, or otherwise, without express written permission of the publisher.

For my late mama P.S. Ranganathan,
my parents Sudha Raman and C.R. Raman,
for enabling me to imbibe in letter and spirit the knowledge that
Bhagavat Sankalpam (divine determination) shapes our lives.

He was my North, my South, my East and West,
My working week and my Sunday rest,
My noon, my midnight, my talk, my song;
I thought that love would last for ever: I was wrong.

The stars are not wanted now: put out every one;
Pack up the moon and dismantle the sun;
Pour away the ocean and sweep up the wood;
For nothing now can ever come to any good.

—W.H. Auden, 'Funeral Blues'

Contents

Foreword: The Luminous Radiance of Self-discovery   xi

PART I

Collapse and Chaos	3
Drowned in Grief	8
The Reality Check	20
Through Potholes to Possibilities	27
The Gift of Grief	33

PART II

Connecting with Carla	47
The 4S's: Stigma, Shame, Secrecy and Silence	53
Owning Our Stories	61
The 3C's: Courage, Compassion and Connection	64
Making Meaning of Suicide Loss	66
A Beautiful World	73
From Pain to Purpose	75

PART III

A Mother's Search for Meaning	87
No Time to Say Goodbye	94

The Neglected Mourner	100
The Psychiatrist as a Survivor of Suicide Loss	106
Playing Hide and Seek with Sorrow	111
Redefining Resilience	116
Grief Cast in Plaster of Paris	121

PART IV

The Right to Grieve	127
What to Say and What Not to Say	132
Mind Your Language, Please	136
The Elusive New Normal	143
Transforming through Trauma	149
Radical Self-care for Survivors	156
The Oyster and the Pearl	161
Churning the Ocean of Grief	166

Afterword

Practical and Pioneering	171
Science and Spirituality	173
Looking Truth Straight in the Eye	175
Fired by Purpose	177
Bibliography	179
Heartfelt Gratitude	184

Foreword

The Luminous Radiance of Self-discovery

Human life is fragile. When the scaffolding of our lives disintegrates and hope is sucked from the marrow of life, thoughts of ending it surface. Albert Camus said, 'Come to terms with death. Thereafter anything is possible,' but that is easier said than done, especially when a person close to you dies by suicide.

The statistics about suicide are cold, hard numbers. Further, much of the literature on suicide is about demography, predisposing factors and psychiatric aspects. There has been very little or no public conversation around survivors of suicide loss. As a result, there is a striking absence of professional and public engagement with suicide loss survivors.

The suddenness of Nandini's loss and her feeling of utter disorientation and dislocation is akin to that of Joan Didion, as articulated in her book *The Year of Magical Thinking*. In an attempt to make sense of the ensuing range of emotions and the vortex of memories, Nandini began to explore the literature on loss and grief associated with suicide and found surprisingly little. The most illuminating insights actually come from within her.

For survivors of suicide loss, there is a fracturing of personal continuity in life. Previously secure coordinates suddenly seem frail. The struggle is to work through these ruptures and weave the broken threads of life into a new and meaningful narrative. The process of scripting an alternative narrative through recuperation can often be arduous and demanding.

It is remarkable that Nandini has been able to navigate her travels in the valley of fear, self-hatred and despair with such perseverance, courage and ingenuity. This book is a dialectical discourse of the author's inner strength in times of overwhelming adversity. The very act of writing about it is an honest and courageous task.

Suicide loss survivors often feel responsible for the act, experience a sense of abandonment and perceive rejection. In narrating her journey beyond suicide, the author has drawn attention to the importance of support groups in providing a space for sharing such experiences and swapping stories to construct new meanings for loss.

This is an exceptional book which documents the pains and lacerations of existence after the loss of a loved one, and the process of healing through renewal and self-affirmation. It is a remarkable piece of writing, at once utterly compelling, deeply affecting and emotionally truthful. It unflinchingly describes emotions that are often not articulated. Her ability to give voice to the suffering of suicide loss survivors, which is often enmeshed in silence, is remarkable. The luminous radiance of self-discovery shines through each page.

In the words of J.R.R. Tolkien:

> From the ashes a fire shall be woken,
> A light from the shadows shall spring;
> Renewed shall be blade that was broken ...

R. Raguram

R. Raguram is a senior consultant psychiatrist and former professor of Psychiatry at the National Institute of Mental Health and Neurosciences (NIMHANS).

PART I

Collapse and Chaos

> Suicide kills two.
> —Dr C.R. Kannan

That was the night my life changed forever. I was travelling by train from Chennai to Madurai, and for some strange reason, I was unable to sleep. I suspected it was because I was eager to get home to my husband Murali and, of course, Malli and Minnal, our two adorable dogs. I surfed the internet aimlessly to pass the time. Vinod Khanna, one of my favourite Bollywood actors, had just passed away. Memories of my teenage hero swamped me. I was lulled to sleep eventually by the unforgettable songs from his films playing in my mind.

The restlessness of the previous night evaporated as the first rays of the summer morning streaked the sky. Dhananjayan, our driver for more than two decades, drove me home. As I neared our house, I called Murali on his cell phone. He usually responded promptly to my call and would be at the door waiting for me. However, that day, he did not answer the phone. Perhaps he had been tired the previous night and overslept, I thought. But after eight calls went unanswered, I sensed that something was wrong. Quelling my gnawing sense of foreboding, I swung into action. I banged on the bedroom window and screamed, 'Murali! Open the door!'

Silence. Despite the summer morning, a thin veil of mist draped itself around me. I shivered, trying to huddle into the comfort of my own skin. I jumped onto the parapet and peered into the bedroom. The light was on, the duvet lay crumpled on the bed, and I could see Murali's phone—its screen flashed once more as I called him yet again in desperation.

'Dhananjayan! Something is wrong.'

He looked at me, stunned. His eyes seemed vacant.

'Let's break into the house,' I declared.

He nodded mutely, following me like a lamb. The massive teak front door was locked.

'Let's try the back door,' I said, ready with Option B.

Meanwhile, Malli, our Golden Retriever, and Minnal, our Rajapalayam, had run into the backyard, overjoyed to see me. Yet, they both seemed agitated. I comforted them, promising to come back and spend time with them in a while. Dhananjayan and I pushed against the French windows that opened onto the beautiful garden. To our surprise, the door yielded. I sprinted towards the bedroom. 'Murali! Murali?' I called, my voice tinged with panic.

The silence was ominous. Cruising on auto pilot, I opened the bedroom door. Murali was not in bed. Gingerly, I moved towards the bathroom. I stood tentatively at the entrance and involuntarily steadied myself before throwing the door open.

Murali was sprawled on the bathroom floor. He was lying on his side, with his face resting on his shoulder. My eyes traversed the length of his body and paused at his hands which were covered in surgical gloves. Bright, gleaming metal instruments—which I immediately recognised as surgical, the tools of his vocation—were embedded like arrows in the crook of his arm.

Space dissolved. Time stood still. The axis of my life heaved, cracked and split.

My eyes widened and I drew my hands towards my mouth, dwarfed by the sheer magnitude of the tragedy. I couldn't quite take in the reality of what I was seeing, but I knew it was all over. My Murali was dead. I lingered by his body, taking in the sadness on his face, which will forever be engraved in my memory.

I closed the bathroom door with a weary finality. 'Dhananjayan, Doctor is dead,' I announced. *'Neenga parunga.* Just check once again, will you?'

Dhananjayan, who was hovering in the background like a frightened child, mustered all the courage he had and walked into the bathroom. After a few seconds, his screams pierced the air. 'Ayyo, Madam! *Poye poytaru.* He has left us forever,' he cried.

'Murali, why did you do this?' I asked, tears running down my cheeks. My agony reverberated through the deathly stillness that was now a strong, silent presence in the house. *'Poda,* how can I live without you?'

Dhananjayan and I wept like orphaned children. Later, he would tell me that he closed Murali's eyes, which were wide open when I discovered his body.

I closed the bathroom and the bedroom doors and trudged wearily to the drawing room. Blinded by tears and choked with grief, I dialled the number for Dr C. Ramasubramanian—better known as Dr CRS—a reputed Madurai-based psychiatrist and close family friend.

Slivers of early morning pink began to streak the summer sky when I called my mother. I dreaded breaking the news to my unsuspecting parents who had just seen me off the previous night. Amma's phone rang for a long time. This would be the most devastating call she would have received in the seven decades of her life, I thought.

'Ma, Murali is dead. Suicide!' I said to her like a distraught child.

'What?' She paused, then said, 'Kanna, we are leaving immediately. Surrender to Sri Lakshmi Narasimha. He will always be with you. Even in this darkest hour.'

My mother's unconditional surrender to the divine had guided me through multiple turbulent crises. This, however, was the litmus test.

Dr and Mrs CRS arrived a few minutes after my phone call.

'Murali's gone! The illness won,' I sobbed. For the two of us, the physician and the caregiver, it was a moment frozen in time.

Meanwhile, the news went viral on social media. My phone rang non-stop. The medical community across India was shocked and incredulous—one of their brightest stars had disappeared forever.

Murali's colleagues, present and former, began to stream in. Many of them made a beeline to the bathroom. I said to Dr Vikhram Ramasubramanian, a young psychiatrist and my former student in school, 'Vikku, please see that Murali is not a photo exhibit. His dignity is as important to me as it was to him.'

He cordoned off inquisitive onlookers and took control of the situation.

Less than a week ago, I had been cleaning the fridge while chatting with Murali, who sat at the dining table on the chair that was closest to me.

'You know, I am not doing anything on purpose. The neurotransmitters in my brain sometimes go awry.'

I looked up momentarily as my hands paused. 'Of course! Never for a moment have I doubted that.'

Murali's face lit up. His smile was endearingly childlike.

That was the last conversation we had. I rehash it endlessly, revelling in it each time. To me, it is an anthem to our enduring bond—it was his 'thank you' to me for having loved and supported him unconditionally.

On 24 April 2017, I was leaving for Chennai for a few days. On an impulse, I rustled up paneer korma and silky soft phulkas,

Murali's favourites. He rolled his eyes appreciatively as he wolfed down his meal. That was the last time I cooked for him.

He gave me a long to-do list that included getting his favourite pickles, condiments, sweets and snacks. An important item on the list was to remake the gold chain my grandmother had given him on our wedding. 'Be sure to get this done immediately. And no excuses that you had no time.' He also gave me a gold nugget and told me to get myself a piece of jewellery. It was a delightful surprise. As he saw me off at the gate, his eyes lingered over me tentatively. A slight smile framed his lips, and his eyes lit up with a soft glow, as they always did when he smiled. His lips twitched as if to say something, then receded like an unwilling wave. I gave him a quick hug and promised to be back 'in just two days'. As I latched the gate, he stood silhouetted on the porch. It was the last time I saw him alive.

In Chennai, I had bought him a beige linen shirt from Indian Terrain, remembering that his birthday was just a few days away. That was my parting gift for him, a shirt that I would drape over his lifeless body when it returned from the mortuary, shrouded and unrecognisable.

Today, three years later, I am unable to cook, or sleep in the old bedroom.

27 April was the day one suicide killed two. That was the day I lost my precious partner and the sun plunged into darkness.

Drowned in Grief

> Your pain is the breaking of the shell that encloses your understanding.
>
> —Khalil Gibran, 'On Pain'

The next forty-eight hours were a free fall into the abyss of the unknown. For the first time in recent years, I felt fearful. In the absence of physical danger, what was I afraid of? I was afraid of the unknown, the loss of predictability and the looming uncertainty.

In *A Grief Observed*, C.S. Lewis writes, 'No one ever told me that grief feels so much like fear.' Grief disrupts the very fabric of our lives. My life ruptured at the seams, and I was haemorrhaging. Could my pain be cauterised? In a nanosecond, all the familiar landmarks in my life had been swept away by oceanic grief.

Until 27 April 2017, suicide was something that happened to others. I naively presumed that it could not happen to me, it could not happen in *my* family. My only brush with suicide had been news reports in the media and the suicide of a friend's parent. Even then, as a young girl, it had struck me that my friend's family refused to discuss it. The death was cloaked in an iron curtain of secrecy, shame and silence.

Ironically, here I was, confronting the suicide of my spouse in our home. I was overcome by the same sense of shame I had witnessed in my friend's family years ago. What would I tell the family? What would I tell my friends? Would they judge Murali, think of him as a criminal? Would they judge me as having failed in my wifely duties?

After all, if I were a responsible, committed wife, I should have seen it coming and prevented it, right? Besides, I was away, travelling on work, when it happened. I began to evolve a strategy, an official version of his death (prolonged illness, sudden death, whatever I deemed might be socially acceptable). A cocktail of toxic emotions throttled me—shame, fear, guilt, anger and remorse. In the days that followed, they would ambush me with the stealth and ruthlessness of an apex predator.

For a few minutes, for just a few minutes, there were only two of us in the house—myself and the lifeless body of Murali. In those moments, before the world descended on us, I decided to speak the truth. I am a communications professional and a gender and diversity advocate who works with LGBTQIA+ issues; I am no stranger to stigma. I realised that choosing not to talk about it would be contributing to the stigma, shame, secrecy and silence around suicide.

I telephoned Sri Guru Rohit Arya, my spiritual guru. In the Vedantic spiritual tradition, a guru dispels the darkness of ignorance. Empathetic and compassionate, Sri Guru assured me of divine guidance and support in the turbulent times ahead. He said, 'Avoid the victim trap. Instead of asking, "Why me?" ask, "Why not me?". What makes you think you are so special that you did not deserve this?'

His wise advice was a mantra, a talisman that cast a protective cocoon over me. In the days ahead, when well-meaning friends and relatives said to me, 'Oh! You didn't deserve this,' I knew better—my journey from victim to survivor had already begun.

The police swarmed the house as uninvited guests, armed with a strong sense of entitlement. Violated as I already was, in the next few days, every shred of my dignity and privacy was breached—all in the name of procedural formalities. In their view, a crime had occurred, and they were determined to ferret out the truth and nab the culprit. Ironically, the deceased victim was also the culprit.

Their needle of suspicion swung towards me. Unlike other kinds of bereavement, a person bereaved by suicide often has to deal with additional stressors, like police investigation, at a time when they are at their most vulnerable.

The police began their endless rounds of interrogations. I often had to answer the same set of questions multiple times. Did I not deserve to be treated with dignity and respect, I wondered. However, the police affirmed they were only 'doing their duty'. I learnt that every death by suicide is regarded as a homicide until proved otherwise.

'Where did you and your husband sleep? In the same room or separate rooms?' asked one policeman, leering at me.

'Same room, of course,' I bristled.

'I heard he was depressed.'

'Yes.'

'Then how come he operated on a patient yesterday?'

How could I explain to him that Murali's standards of professional excellence were uncompromising? That for him, patients were primary, and everyone—including himself—was secondary? That paradoxically, he, who was such a compassionate surgeon, never had an iota of self-compassion?

The policeman triumphantly produced a sheaf of papers from a folder in his hand. 'Here! This is a letter from your husband for you!'

My heart danced joyously at the sight of Murali's familiar neat handwriting that seemed to leap from the pages, crackling with energy. I lunged forward and snatched the papers. I held them close to my heart and kissed them all over. For a moment, it was difficult to believe that this was the last communication I would receive from the person with whom I had shared over three decades of my life. Murali was a prolific letter writer, and this was his final epistolary indulgence.

Addressing me as 'Nandini dear', he said that his 'problem' had become insurmountable of late. The coherence and clarity of thought and expression in the letter were remarkable. He even detailed our finances and specified my inheritance.

Murali was always hyper-responsible. And it showed in his last act of love and concern for me. Unlike some partners, he did not leave me in financial distress. The last line—'Sorry. Sorry. Deeply sorry'—is forever branded in letters of fire in my heart. In the Hindu tradition, this is known as *kshama yachanam*—begging forgiveness. In asking for forgiveness, Murali had elevated himself.

Today, two years later, the letter still remains a cherished piece of communication from him. It also serves as a legal document, which is why I've stashed it away securely in a bank locker. Whenever I visit the locker, I read and reread it. He is vivified in the letter, cryopreserved for me, like an insect fossilised in amber. Every time I read it, I dissolve into a flood of tears.

Suicide notes can often be a lifeline—the last link with the deceased victim, tethering the survivor of the loss to a world whose doors are forever closed to him or her. Most survivors of suicide loss I have interacted with wish that their loved one had left behind a letter for them. Suicidologists have observed that only a minority of suicide victims leave notes—less than one in four among adults and fewer still among teenagers.[1] However, not all suicide notes are heartfelt or filled with gratitude; some can be vindictive, revengeful and even spiteful, casting aspersions—real or imagined—on survivors of the loss.

---

[1] Ronald W. Maris, Alan L. Berman and Morton M. Silverman, *Comprehensive Textbook of Suicidology* (Guilford Press, 2000).

Murali's letter was not dated. For a person who was meticulous and precise, I couldn't believe this was a mere oversight. I wondered when he had written it; this was one of the many questions that would remain unanswered. Suicide notes are the last words from the deceased, usually written in the final moments before the fatal act. However, in Murali's instance, I suspected he had begun the letter a few days before he died, and had provided the finishing touches and the last sign off just minutes before his carefully orchestrated final exit. While it is simplistic to place the suicide note in a restricted time frame, in reality, it represents the culmination of years of distorted thinking and emotional pain, aptly described by the well-known suicidologist Edwin Shneidman as 'psych ache'.

From my perspective as a communications professional, the irony of the suicide letter hit me hard. It is well known that communication is dyadic and loops itself non-linearly between the sender and the receiver. But in this case, while Murali conveyed his sense of helplessness and hopelessness and his seemingly 'insurmountable' problems, how was I to give him feedback or complete the dyadic communication? It was one-way communication, a cul de sac.

Later, when I began to read extensively on suicide, this sentence, by Shneidman, made a lot of sense to me: 'Suicide notes are cryptic maps of ill-advised journeys.' Today, I know that it is impossible to understand what is going on in the mind of a person with suicidal ideation. One can never know with certainty why they did what they did. Their inner landscape is complex and cryptic; we do not have the keys to decode their maps or their journeys. This realisation is both humbling and liberating.

Meanwhile, the trickle of visitors turned into a flood. When I look back on those forty-eight hours, I think of myself as cruising on auto pilot. There were arrangements to be made for the funeral, legalities to be attended to, friends and relatives to be informed.

Among the most painful tasks for me was drafting Murali's obituary notice to be inserted in the following day's English and Tamil newspapers. I was blinded by tears as my stiff fingers reluctantly punched the keyboard. 'When someone you love becomes a memory, that memory becomes a treasure.'

Just yesterday, Murali had been an embodied *atma*, the higher self, I thought, but today he has almost acquired framed-photograph status. As Murali's body was being taken to the mortuary for autopsy, I refused to look, instead shutting myself in my study and clinging to Malli and Minnal, sobbing uncontrollably. They, too, were distressed, agitated by my tears. Malli placed her cushioned paws on me and licked my cheeks. In the next few months, even when I cried silently (and there was not a single day in the first year when I did not cry), Malli became my 24/7 on-call therapist with her wet nose.

I will never forget what Murali looked like when they brought him back from the mortuary. He was a tall person who loomed larger than life, and it seemed as if death had diminished and shrunk him to unrecognisable dimensions. I sobbed my heart out when I saw him bundled in a beige handwoven shroud. Yet, there was something ascetic and spartan about him that even death could not obliterate or erase. It was as if he was defying death in what was his last hurrah.

'Why did you do this? Was my love not enough for you?' I sobbed as I threw myself at the coffin. Impulsively, I rushed inside the house and came back with the beige linen shirt I had bought for him. I draped it on the coffin. A crowd had gathered, but to me, it seemed as if there was no one there except Murali and I. Only later did I recall hearing sobs and sniffles from those around me.

Although Murali was bereft of the *prana*, life force, that animates a person, I still could not bring myself to refer to him as a 'body'. Sridhar Vadhyar, the priest who had arrived to perform the funeral ceremony and rites, was a silent witness to my outpouring of grief. He later told me that my eulogy brought him to tears, touching a chord within him and breaking his professional demeanour. He told me, 'When *perumal* (god) wanted a *vaidhyar* (physician) for himself, he chose Dr Murali.' He remained a sensitive and humane presence throughout that first year of my loss, when he visited to perform the monthly death rituals, acting as a source of solace and support. He encouraged me to find joy and meaning in work and to engage with nature to reclaim myself. Such sensitivity and compassion from religious stakeholders can make a huge difference to people bereaved by suicide.

Unmindful of the people around me and uncaring of whether I would be perceived as theatrical, I allowed myself to be immersed in grief at the funeral. I knew I had to embrace my grief and surrender unconditionally to it in order to heal.

The crowd of friends and relatives had swelled into a tide. That day, all of Madurai was mourning for the 'good doctor' who had touched so many lives with his gift of healing. He was deluged with floral tributes, which prompted someone to remark that there were no more rose garlands in the city that day. However, even at the funeral, I intuitively sensed people's reactions to the idea of bereavement by suicide. Living in a death-phobic and grief-denying culture makes most people uncomfortable while visiting a bereaved person. While some people were genuinely empathic and concerned for me, others were not. For many, I was an object of curiosity, conjecture and pity. People gathered in knots and talked in hushed whispers. When they saw me, they lapsed into an embarrassed silence.

A few people felt entitled to interrogate me. 'Why did he kill himself?' 'Didn't you see it coming?' 'Why did you leave him alone that day?' My response was a stony silence.

Survivors of suicide loss are confronted with multiple challenges: relentless speculation, public gaze, intrusive probing and insensitivity. These factors compound our primary loss and make our grief inordinately complex. Had Murali died due to 'acceptable' reasons such as a terminal illness, cardiac arrest or an accident, I am certain that I would not have come under a moral scanner. As I discovered painfully in the immediate aftermath of the tragedy and the succeeding months, there is enormous blaming and shaming of survivors of suicide loss, especially of the victim's parents and wives.

More probing questions followed, with complete disregard and insensitivity, a stark violation of the rights of both the bereaved and the deceased to privacy and dignity. 'Shut up! I am grieving! Why should I give you explanations? How does it help?' I wanted to scream at those who questioned me. I felt naked, vulnerable and fragile. Gradually, as if osmotically, I too began to internalise the shame and began to blame myself. Was there anything I *could* have done to prevent it? Deep down, though, I knew the truth—I had been a wonderfully supportive and caring partner.

A senior member of the family suggested that I 'hush it up' and pass Murali's death off as a non-suicidal death. That was the shame and stigma of suicide having its say. Another relative accused me of murder. Others took it upon themselves to get to the root of the matter by interrogating my domestic help and the driver about what had *really* happened. I often wonder if their findings disappointed them.

I wanted to shield myself from the accusatory glances and shy away from the needle of blame and shame that was swinging wildly towards me. The barbs of stigma need not always be verbal, explicit or tangible. They deliver venom even through evocative body language, in silences and pauses. For many people, the occasion was a perfect opportunity to speculate about the cause of suicide. They didn't seem to know that it is simplistic and naive to reduce the cause of suicide to a single reason, however compelling it may be. Suicide is a complex phenomenon precipitated by a cluster of biophysical and psychosocial factors. Understandably, however, neither they nor I could sift fact from fiction that day.

Later, I would realise that this discomfort about the cause of the death, their unwillingness to be unconditionally supportive of me by validating my grief, and their tendency to speculate and gossip about why it had happened were all part of the stigma that shrouds suicide. That was my first experience of it. Over the next year, I would encounter it in various forms, shapes and sizes. I had not realised that stigma could be protean, like an amoeba transforming itself or like water assuming the shape of its container. It is not one-size-fits-all.

Murali's funeral was solemn and poignant. He was laid in the living room. When the last visitor of the day left, it was well past midnight. I drifted rather unwillingly into a sedative-induced sleep that night, desperately wishing I could plunge into a slumber from which I need never wake up. But the early light of the morning sun stung me awake like an astringent spritzed on my face. My head was throbbing wildly, and I was dazed—the shock of grief had an anaesthetic effect, numbing and blunting my emotions, only to erupt with volcanic force when it wore off a little.

The funeral ceremonies began around eight o'clock in the morning. I had every right to perform my husband's last rites according to the Hindu Dharma Shastras. Impulsively, I wore the rose garland meant for Murali, as I imagined myself to be Andal, the Earth Goddess, who offered a garland to Rangammanar, whom she regarded as her divine partner. Andal, my favourite deity, who embodies the divine feminine, is the presiding deity of the famous Srivilliputhur temple, fifty kilometres from Madurai. 'See, Murali, look at me!' I implored, hoping to evoke bridal nostalgia. He would have turned sixty the following year, the age at which it is customary to have one's wedding ritual re-enacted. I had wanted to have a small, private function at the Andal temple to observe the occasion.

Did tears of sorrow have the power to restore life? Like Savitri, I too wanted to implore Death to bring Murali back to life

'Yes, I can restore him to life,' Death answered, 'but *he* does not want to live. We have to respect his decision. How can you decide for him? Each of us scripts our destiny based on the choices we make. It was his choice. Let him go peacefully.'

I nodded through the haze. Yama, the God of Death, is the fountain of wisdom.

'I'll wait for you. Forever,' I whispered. It seemed impossible to let go. With unwilling hands, I removed the garland and draped it over his lifeless body. Thirty-one years ago, when we exchanged garlands, could I have imagined that, one day, I would be re-enacting the bridal scene, dyed in the warp and weft of my sorrow?

Murali's body was lifted by four pallbearers, and he began his last journey. 'Don't go, don't leave me behind!' I wept.

For a few days after death, the departed *atma* hovers above the body and is a mute witness to the outpourings of grief. I wondered if my grief would make him want to return. Perhaps I had not revealed to him how much I would miss him and had portrayed myself as a strong, independent person who could cope with anything that life threw at her. 'This is one situation where you overestimated me!' I lamented.

He was laid in the portico for the final rites before he left home, never to return. I brought Malli and Minnal to say goodbye to the person they had adored, and who in turn had loved them dearly. I expected them to lick him and jump on him, as they usually did. However, they both sniffed him ever so briefly and instantly turned their faces away. In their animal wisdom, they knew that his *prana* was gone; the person they loved was no longer present. This was a lifeless, inert body. As far as they were concerned, it was a clean break with the past.

Usually, when I called out Murali's name, both of them would perk up their ears and a look of recognition would animate their faces. I knelt before them and whispered, 'Murali.' No response. No look of recognition. As far as they were concerned, Murali was gone. They were yogic in their response. To this day, I wonder at the uncanny ability of animals to discern the metaphysical.

The journey to the crematorium was the longest and most painful I've ever had to undertake. We drove past familiar landmarks in the city which, in the past twenty-seven years, had become home to us. When the cortège passed the hospital where Murali had last worked, I saw that the entire contingent of doctors and nursing staff had lined the streets to pay silent homage to their star doctor.

The last rites at the crematorium had a certain finality about them. I circumambulated the body and respectfully prostrated before Murali. 'Sorry,' I said. 'I did my best for you. If there were lapses, it was unintended. The whole of AIIMS is missing you; they called to tell me so. We are all missing you already. My life will never be the same again. I love you.'

The fire urn was alight with blazing flames. With the sacred fire as witness, we had married. The same sacred fire now sealed the dissolution of the marriage by engulfing the mortal remains of one partner.

I had kept the marriage vows made with the sacred fire as witness. For better or worse, through triumphs and hardships, joys and sorrows, Murali and I were two individuals yoked to each other karmically. Now it was time for the karmic knot to unravel itself.

'Your paths are different. Even though a man and woman are married, their individual karma and their individual journeys are solitary and divergent,' said my guru. His words, as always, were wise. I recalled them in that moment.

'Goodbye, Murali. You've been my greatest teacher,' I said as he was slid into the electric crematorium and the door closed with a metallic clang of finality. '*Om namo Narayana! Om namo Narayana,*' I continued to chant, praying that Murali's *atma* would rest in eternal peace, cradled in the lap of divine love.

In a few seconds, the body was reduced to ashes. Soon, he would be an inextricable part of the Pancha Bhootas, the five primal elements—earth, fire, water, air and ether.

On the way back home, I felt numb. After the intense drama of the last two days, my mind was deceptively calm. When I entered our home, the space felt empty. From that day onwards, I would have to get used to returning to a home without Murali. I felt as though a large part of me had been amputated.

Malli and Minnal were upset and clung to me when I returned. I sat them down and talked to them, as advised by my guru, who insisted that the dogs needed to be 'told of the transition'. 'Malli, Minnal … Murali is dead. He has gone to a place from where he will bless us, protect us and continue to play with us. When it's our time to go, we'll all meet him across the rainbow bridge. I want the three of us to be together. I'll always look after both of you,' I whispered, as they nuzzled against me. From that instant onwards, they were calm, peaceful and relaxed—back to their frisky, bubbly selves. Perhaps they had been waiting to hear this from me. From now on, it would be just the three of us.

Dr CRS said to me, 'One chapter in your life, that of a wife, is over. However, there are many more glorious chapters waiting to be written.'

One chapter in my life was certainly over, but I wondered if I would continue to read and reread that chapter. Would the past hold me hostage? Or would I be able to honour the past and use it as a springboard to rebuild my life? Why had this happened? That day, I had no answers. Only questions.

The Reality Check

The death of a significant other by suicide is a stressor of unparalleled magnitude in most people's lives and even the most psychologically mature individual may encounter difficulty in responding to it.

—Edward J. Dunne in *Suicide and Its Aftermath: Understanding and Counseling the Survivors*

The Oxford English Dictionary defines a widow as a woman whose husband has died (and who has not remarried). I was not just a widow. I was a widow whose husband had died by suicide.

The Scarlet Letter W for widow dangled like an albatross around my neck. I was determined to wrench it away, to refuse to give up my power to regressive societal norms of womanhood and widowhood. The dictionary may contain the literal or denotative meaning of words. However, any word, in any language, has a host of connotations and associations.

Through my deep engagement with feminism in South Asia, especially in India, I was only too aware of the implications of my new-found status. Although much has changed in terms of how Indian society perceives widowhood, there are several unspoken assumptions that still hold weight. For instance, a widow needs to minimise or downplay herself in terms of the way she dresses and the space she occupies. In my own dignified yet assertive manner, I was determined to reject every one of these disempowering and dehumanising stereotypes.

I did not have to wait too long. When I first left my house, a friend remarked, 'You wear such bright, colourful clothes!'

I replied firmly but politely, 'I am a butterfly. I cannot change into a moth!'

Stony silence met my response.

Another friend said to me, 'You *still* wear your nose ring?'

The jibe was astringent. Did she mean to emphasise my new-found status? Or was it just an insensitive remark that was not intended to hurt? I had no way of knowing for sure. Overburdened with grief, I felt the need to stop seeking explanations for the behaviour of others and, instead, acknowledge my own feelings of hurt. I learnt that intent does not matter as much as impact.

I responded with a tone and demeanour that indicated my surprise at someone like her, modern and well-educated, subscribing to regressive stereotypes such as insisting on marital markers like nose rings being removed after widowhood. In better times, I would have engaged in a conversation that may have helped push boundaries. I would have, perhaps, got her to see that wedding rings and *mangal sutras* are merely external markers of matrimony, that the commitment to a relationship goes much deeper.

I shared this incident with a close friend and told her, 'I am determined to be a glamorous widow.' We roared with laughter. Humour, I was soon to discover, was the best antidote to pain.

Daughter, sister, wife, mother and daughter-in-law are just roles that a woman may take on at different stages of her life. No single one can be equated with her entire identity—her sense of who she fundamentally is. As far as I was concerned, although my role as a wife had ended, my life did not have to end or be minimised or deglamorised because of this. Perhaps, as my friend Usu, a feminist activist from Kenya, would tell me later, being 'strongly grounded in feminist consciousness' was also critical to my healing as a survivor of suicide loss.

Like most women, hadn't I simply gone from being someone's daughter to someone's wife? So, who was I now? My past—largely anchored to my role as the wife of a well-known doctor—had been wrenched from me. The clinical, aseptic world of medicine and surgery that permeated my life were no longer my reality.

As the thirteen-day period of mourning, part of the post-bereavement tradition in my community, drew to a close, I felt like an actor on the proscenium, who takes her final bow at the end of a performance that will never be repeated. There were no encores, no applause, no standing ovation, just silence. Soon, the flood of people who had come to condole me morphed into a trickle and my solitary journey through grief began.

As I sat on the porch, flanked by Malli and Minnal, the metallic wind chimes that Murali had chosen brushed against each other in the gentle breeze. I sensed his presence in the pauses between the chiming, in the silence between the notes. Even today, the tinkle of the wind chimes attunes me to Murali's presence—a wordless comfort for an aching longing.

How was I to navigate the landscape of grief when my internal GPS had crashed? I felt like a cork tossed around in the turbulent ocean of pain, unmoored and unanchored. Ironically, the source of my intense pain also enabled me to touch the core of my being. But with every onslaught of intense emotion—anger, sadness, fear—I became more vulnerable and fragile.

The most difficult part of losing someone you love is not their physical absence but confronting the huge void that stares defiantly and mockingly at you, threatening to destroy you like a raging fire. Could I be in the presence of pain and immerse myself in it? Could I, as one of my favourite poets Oriah Mountain Dreamer put it, 'sit with pain, mine or your own, without moving to hide it, or fade it, or fix it'?

'Suicide can shatter the things you take for granted about yourself, your relationships, and your world,' writes Jack Jordan, clinical psychologist and co-author of *After Suicide Loss: Coping with Your Grief.* He talks about the popular 'flu model' approach. This standard quick-fix attitude to dealing with grief assumes that grief is unpleasant but relatively short-lived. After a stay at home and a period of mourning, the bereaved person is expected to jump back into life. However, when you transpose this to suicidal grief, you encounter even more roadblocks—the stigma, shame, secrecy and silence around suicidal bereavement make the grieving process more complicated.

The silence, in particular, can be deafening. The silence around suicide prevents people, both those at risk and families impacted by suicide, from speaking up and asking for help. The more we choose not to talk about it, the more difficult it becomes to effectively address the problem. How do we shatter this festering collective silence?

We are deeply ashamed to even admit that it was suicide in the first place. Instead, we tend to create 'acceptable' explanations for the cause of death, like, 'It was a heart attack', or provide a similar socially acceptable reason. Can we learn to talk about the sense of shame associated with the act and the people who have died this way? This is neither to glorify suicide nor to condemn it. People who die by suicide are not heroes, nor are they cowards or criminals. Suicide is *not* a crime. It is a public health crisis, a mental health issue that may be treatable and even preventable.

How can we create spaces to change the language we use to talk about suicide, to create shifts in the predominant mindset? This can happen only with the language of love and compassion, not judgement, ignorance and fear.

Grief is the feeling of loss or emptiness when you lose someone precious with whom you were intimately connected. When that person is no longer around, your whole world seems empty. Spousal bereavement, in particular, is associated with high levels of stress. When my maternal grandfather died at the age of ninety, I recall my grandmother grieving intensely for the partner she had spent more than fifty-five years with. Her grief, though understated, was poignant and powerful. She felt forlorn and adrift, as if a vital part of her had gone away with her husband. My grandfather, when alive, had loomed larger than life. He presided over a large extended family, and he was universally adored and respected. We, her immediate and extended family, were unconditionally loving and supportive of her grief.

My grandfather died of ageing-related causes. I discovered, more than three decades later, that a death by suicide does not elicit the same level of compassion. The huge empathy deficit I sensed in most people made me feel isolated, excluded and unloved. Most of our relatives seemed self-absorbed in their grief. They were mourning the loss of someone they loved, and their compassion and concern did not extend to include me beyond a superficial level. Was it because they were so confused by suicide that they did not know how to respond appropriately? Possibly.

The so-called friends were no better. Before Murali's body was sent for post-mortem, the police began their seemingly endless rounds of routine investigations. These even took place in the living room where people had congregated. Feeling violated and vulnerable, I requested the police for privacy and suggested we move to the adjoining room. 'Well! Investigations are investigations! If she has nothing to hide, why is she shying away?' questioned a long-time friend, within my range of hearing. I squirmed.

As an acutely intuitive person, I picked upon the shame and blame that was being levelled at me from all directions. Why were they doing this, I wondered. What had I done to feel ashamed about?

I would often spot vultures during my forays into the wild and marvel at the majestic scavenging birds of prey that descend on carrion. At first, I would spot one raptor, a tiny speck in the distance. But soon, as if impelled by a mysterious force, a colony of vultures would zero in from all directions, digging their talons into the rotting flesh. Even vultures, though, do not prey on live flesh. I have come to believe human raptors are unmatched in their capacity to inflict pain on vulnerable members of their own species.

Why did my so-called friend respond in such a crass manner? I have no answers. I don't believe everyone has to be trained in grief counselling to be able to respond appropriately, for the language of concern and compassion is most certainly universal. Grief itself is a universal experience, not unique to humans. Among mammals, elephants in the wild have elaborate mourning rituals in which the herd collectively supports the bereaved elephant.

My faith in people had already begun to ebb in the days after Murali's death; in the year that followed, it would leach and erode my very being. I had to remind myself that for every person who betrayed my trust, there were sensitive, loving and supportive people whose acts of loving kindness left me speechless with gratitude.

Grief is a visceral, embodied experience. In other words, it's not all in the mind; it's also equally located in the body. While I anticipated the emotional roller coaster of grieving, the physical presence of grief in my body felt intimate and entrenched, and challenged me in every sense. I was enveloped in inertia and lethargy. Even the smallest act seemed Herculean. It was as though grief held me in its talons, like a raptor triumphantly clutching its prey.

I experienced all the physical symptoms of grief: dizzy spells, nausea, vomiting, sleeplessness, an upset stomach, loss of appetite, explosive headaches, chronic fatigue and inability to focus. In addition, I dealt with wildly fluctuating hypertension and headaches that felt like atomic implosions. I was constantly tired and wanted to do nothing but sleep. Yet, when I tried to nap during the day or prepared to sleep at night, sleep eluded me. Finally, when I could not deal with this charade of the body and the mind any longer, I resorted to short-term use of prescription sedatives and anti-depressants that helped me tide over that first, acute phase of grief.

The inability to focus was especially distressing. My attention span was pixelated, like a million dots that form a digital photograph. I felt enveloped in a dense, immovable fog. Does intense grief rewire the neurons in the brain, their connections and interconnections, I wondered. I tried resuming work, but even turning on my laptop required tremendous effort. And when I tried to read, the words did not make sense. I felt as if my synaptic connections had snapped and my IQ had plummeted.

Through Potholes to Possibilities

> It doesn't interest me what planets are squaring your moon. I want to know if you have touched the center of your own sorrow, if you have been opened by life's betrayals or have become shriveled and closed from fear of further pain. I want to know if you can sit with pain, mine or your own, without moving to hide it, or fade it, or fix it.
>
> —Oriah Mountain Dreamer, *The Invitation*

Our darkest moments contain seeds of transformation. At every turning point in my life, I've sought to engage with my challenges by seeking to expand my knowledge and understanding. Informed perspectives have always empowered me. This time was no exception.

I switched on my laptop. My fingers felt leaden, burdened by the crushing weight of sorrow. The screen lit up. As the Google page appeared on my screen, I tentatively typed in 'suicide'. I was impressed when the first link that popped up contained a helpline number for assistance. I skimmed through several sites that talked about suicide—the act of intentionally killing oneself, the signs and symptoms, ways to prevent suicide, and a host of other related topics. A few of the sites had me hooked to the screen. It was as if my brain fog had selectively lifted to absorb something that was to have a profound impact on me. An article titled 'Understanding Survivors of Suicide Loss' jumped out at me from the pages of my favourite psychology magazine, *Psychology Today*.

I paused. What or who were survivors of suicide loss? I had heard of survivors of cancer, being one myself. I wondered if surviving suicide loss was similar. A survivor of suicide loss, I discovered, is someone who has lost a family member or a close friend to suicide. That was my freshly minted status. I was perhaps the newest entrant into an exclusive club, in which membership is always by chance, not choice.

The writer mentions the universality of grief and grieving. However, she writes, suicide is a 'death like no other. ... As such, survivors of suicide loss may encounter blame, judgment or social exclusion—while mourners of loved ones who have died from terminal illness, accident, old age or other kinds of death usually receive sympathy and compassion. It's strange how we would never blame a family member for a loved one's cancer or Alzheimer's, but society continues to cast a shadow on a loved one's suicide.'

It was epiphanic. Something shifted within me when I read the article, and my journey as a survivor of suicide loss began. The discovery anchored me: it validated all the confusing feelings that swamped me. I wondered if I could ever be completely understood by someone who was not a survivor of suicide loss; this is perhaps one instance where comprehension may not be complete without first-hand experience. I suddenly felt alive again. Having been tossed about in a turbulent ocean of grief, I now saw a glimmer of sunshine on the horizon. Was this the new language with which I could rewrite the narrative of my life?

I began to seek more knowledge. Once my intent was clear, I found myself exposed to thousands of webpages. The American Suicidology Association, in particular, helped me understand that 'the primary goal of a suicide is not to end life, but to end pain'.

I also responded to *A Handbook for Survivors of Suicide* by Jeffery Jackson,[1] who had lost his wife to suicide. He writes, 'For the person you lost, the pain is over. Now it's time to start healing

---

[1] www.suicidology.org/wp-content/uploads/2019/07/SOS_handbook.pdf

yours. You are a "survivor of suicide", and as that unwelcome designation implies, your survival—your *emotional* survival—will depend on how well you learn to cope with your tragedy. The bad news: surviving this will be the second worst experience.'

I was shocked, but not surprised, to read that according to the American Psychiatric Association, suicide bereavement was considered 'catastrophic' and on par with a concentration camp experience. Through my research, I learnt to distinguish between the catalyst or triggers of suicide and the condition that led to it.

Suicide is rarely an impulsive decision. Although the final act may seem impulsive, it is often preceded by years of emotional agony and pain. In the early stages of the suicide trajectory, most people who contemplate suicide are ambivalent about it. Remember the classic Hamletian dilemma: to be or not to be? Unlike the case of Hamlet, for people who die by suicide, once the decision is made—which is often the most difficult part—implementing it is not as difficult as it seems.

As I read more about suicide, I connected with Murali's suicide trajectory. On a suicide whodunit, I began to frantically search for answers. When would he have made that all-important decision to call it quits? I began to rehash my memories of him.

His last phone call to Dr CRS on that fateful night, an hour or so before he died, had ended on a note of fun and laughter. They were to meet the next morning at our home. Dr CRS had requested dosa for breakfast.

'Plain or ghee roast?' Murali had asked.

'Ghee roast,' Dr CRS had said. He was the last person to hear Murali's voice.

I still wonder what could have happened after that phone call. Was it a decoy? A red herring? Had Murali already decided to end it all and his phone call was a 'thank you' to his close friend and psychiatrist for whom he had deep respect, and who had, by then, treated him for bipolar depression for over a decade and a half?

Malli always slept with us. On that fateful night, however, she was outside. I was sure Murali had let her out late at night. What were his thoughts as he did so? Was his mind already made up? Did he give her a last hug and kiss her goodbye? Did he bid farewell to little Minnal, whom he had brought home just a few months back?

Were his last strides to the bathroom purposeful? If I had spoken to him then, would it have made a difference? Could I have prevented the act? Or had I just been pressing the pause button for the past thirty years? Did Murali think of me as he let his life ebb out of his body? Abandoning someone who loved and cared for him with every bit of her being—wasn't that the ultimate act of betrayal? Or was it the only way he knew to end his pain? I knew I would only have endless questions, not answers. Like every survivor of suicide loss, I was desperate to decode the undecodable.

'Attempting to decipher precisely the thoughts of the suicide victim is much like trying to understand a foreign language by eavesdropping on a conversation. You can analyse the sounds and syllables all day long, but it's not likely you're going to understand much of what was said,' writes Jackson in *A Handbook for Survivors of Suicide*.

Is suicide then a matter of choice, I asked myself. Or a choiceless choice? 'Choice implies that a suicidal person can reasonably look at alternatives and select among them. If they could rationally choose, it would not be suicide. Suicide happens when ... no other choices are seen,' writes Adina Wrobleski in *Suicide—Why? 85 Questions and Answers about Suicide*.

All of next year, I spent almost every minute of my waking hours glued to the internet. I was in the grip of an insatiable need to glean as much as possible about this crushing catastrophe. By now, I had read everything relevant to the topic, downloaded every PDF and re-read it many times over. I was now fluent in the vocabulary, syntax and lexicon of suicide. My newly acquired role as a self-styled suicidologist was taking shape.

Around the same time, I discovered another new term: postvention services for survivors of suicide loss. This refers to activities which reduce risk and promote healing after a suicide death. According to research, family members of individuals who die by suicide, including parents, children and siblings, are at increased risk of suicide—almost 400 times higher than others. 'Picture a suicide death as a pebble dropped in a pond. While the first and biggest waves hit the family and those closest to the decedent, the impact spreads outward to others exposed to the death such as friends, witnesses, first responders, treatment providers, and colleagues,' says the Suicide Prevention Resource Center.[2]

Knowledge by itself stagnates. To make a tangible impact, it needs to be transmuted through action. Exactly a month after Murali's death, I travelled to Coimbatore for the launch of a textbook on operative spinal surgery by Dr J.K.B.C. Parthiban, a well-known Coimbatore-based neurosurgeon. At the event, I spoke about my experience with multiple spine surgeries, four of which were on my lower back. Against seemingly insurmountable odds, Dr Parthiban had done a miraculous fourth surgery with fantastic outcomes. Murali had been a pillar of support and strength during my long tryst with spine surgeries. Ironically, he had also been scheduled to speak at the function. I was overcome with emotion. Before an audience of nearly 200 people, I spoke about my journey and my recent loss and the need to reconstruct my life. It was my first experience of talking in public about being a survivor of suicide loss.

I received a standing ovation. The stigma, shame and secrecy of suicide were non-issues now. The road ahead was paved with possibilities, not potholes and pitfalls. Then, Dr Parthiban sprang

---

[2] www.sprc.org/news/postvention-prevention

a surprise by requesting me to inaugurate the conference, along with his wife Harini Parthiban. His gesture touched me, feminist as it was in letter and spirit.

The Coimbatore experience filled me with hope and a sense of renewal, although life, as I had known it, had irretrievably vanished. I am a naturally brave and resilient person. Murali had always admired these qualities in me. My long engagement with illness and my steadfast support and love for him had convinced him that I could 'handle anything with grace'. There were times when I wondered if he had overestimated my resilience. This was a tough ordeal by anyone's standards, including mine.

The Gift of Grief

> Embrace your grief; for there your soul will grow.
> —Carl Jung

I've always disliked militaristic metaphors that describe dealing with life's challenges as a battle, a crusade or a war to be won, with the enemy either subdued or conquered. There is an unnecessary belligerence to it. Throughout my life, I've dealt with challenges by empowering myself with knowledge. I read extensively about the challenges I had to negotiate—infertility, multiple spine surgeries and thyroid cancer. I read obsessively, and books continue to be my life support when dealing with crises. Knowledge widens my perspectives, enriches me with nuanced insights and offers me a wide-angle view. This time too, books were a lifeline despite the fact that I sensed a radical departure from my habitual ways of responding.

In contrast to an all-in-the-head purely mental approach, comprehensible and ultimately conquerable by knowledge and intellect, I experienced grief in multiple sites in the body—the heart, the stomach, the head, in every one of the trillions of cells. It had a feral rawness, a ferocity, an intensity that overwhelmed and humbled me.

Love and loss, I discovered, are two sides of the same coin. The more intense the love, the more poignant the loss. Traversing the landscape of grief is a solitary journey. There are no maps, guides, manuals or GPS.

A few years ago, the death of Goldie, my Golden Retriever, had been my first apprenticeship with sorrow. Goldie and I were twin flames. I had been travelling on work to Hyderabad when she died. For thirteen years, she had been my personal therapist, companion and foot warmer all rolled into one. Life without Goldie was unimaginable, and at her passing, I experienced intense grief that threatened to destabilise me.

A compassionate psychotherapist told me then, 'Don't fight grief. Instead, surrender to it. Touch the bottom of your sorrow and you will surface whole and healed.'

In retrospect, Goldie's death was a curtain raiser for the serial losses I would experience in the next two years. Six months after Goldie died, her companion Scooby Doo, a Doberman, followed her. And Murali followed Scooby six months later. The serial losses that culminated in Murali's death enabled me to embrace and affirm my vulnerability. Vulnerability, I discovered, is strength. The well-known psychotherapist Francis Weller talks of the sacredness of grief and the grieving process. In his classic, *The Wild Edge of Sorrow: Rituals of Renewal and the Sacred Work of Grief*, he writes with poetic sensitivity and compassionate insight based on decades of experience with grief and loss, 'Every one of us must undertake an apprenticeship with sorrow. We must learn the art and craft of grief, discover the profound ways it ripens and deepens us. While grief is an intense emotion, it is also a skill we develop through a profound walk with loss. Facing grief is hard work. ... It takes outrageous courage to face outrageous loss. This is precisely what we are being called to do.'

Something within me began to shift. The first shift happened the day after Murali's funeral. I found it painful to look at his clothes and other belongings stacked in the cupboards. Spontaneously, I decided to give them away to people who might be able to use them. After all, it is people who are precious: we treasure memories, we cherish moments, and these are independent of any objects. I know there are people who hold on to the artefacts of their departed loved ones even years after they have passed on, but it was different for me.

Just a couple of days after the funeral, I discovered a treasure. I was clearing out old papers when something slipped out of a bunch of notepads. It was a piece of paper covered with an unfamiliar handwriting in red ink. 'There is no light which cannot pervade you,' it said. I couldn't make out the scrawled signature. I asked several of my friends who I thought were capable of writing something as profound as this message. But I have still not been able to identify the mysterious person who thought it wise to slip in such a message, confident that I would stumble upon it if I was meant to. I framed the paper, and it now occupies a prominent place in my living room—a constant reminder that darkness can never obliterate light.

Murali was an inveterate collector. While he had exquisite taste, he had developed the habit, of late, of hoarding junk that cluttered the house and blocked energy. In his last letter, he had requested me to 'clear the junk'. Over the next month, driven by a demonic energy, I began to clean the house. I must have cleared cartloads of things, though I retained all that was beautiful. I then moved things around. I shifted the furniture, re-painted the house and acquired a few artefacts to replace those I had given away. Would I be able to do the same with my memories? Trash the painful; cherish the good and the beautiful.

A friend remarked that the changes in my outer life were symbolic of internal shifts taking place within me. I knew that I had just taken baby steps in my long journey through the wilderness of grief. Change is contextual and situational. Transition, however, is psychological. It is an inner response to the change. It involves a reconfiguring of one's inner landscape. 'Without a transition, change is just a rearrangement of furniture,' says William Bridges, author and speaker, whose pioneering work on transition changed my views on how one deals with change. Even the act of rearranging furniture in the early phase of my grief was a sign of hope.

'Any transition serious enough to alter your definition of the self will require not just small adjustments in your way of thinking and living but a full-on metamorphosis,' writes Martha Beck.

In the dark depths of the night, I often held my mother's hand for comfort. She would later tell me that she felt my entire body shivering.

'Ma, we will get out of this, won't we? We have to find our way out.'

'Yes, of course!' she would whisper in the hushed stillness of the night.

Apart from my mother, there was one other person whose words allowed me to see light in the overwhelming darkness. This was my father's younger brother, C.R. Kannan, an eminent US-based endocrinologist who lived in the US. Soon after Murali's death, he wrote me these letters, which I read and reread many times.

> My dear Nandini,
>
> It is almost one week since we had that heart-wrenching conversation regarding your great loss. People always seem to say things happen for a reason. However, I cannot understand how that can be applied to a situation of this magnitude. There is no one to blame except that fickle finger of fate.
>
> You need to know without any ambiguity that you share no guilt, none whatsoever. You have to pick up the pieces and move through the loss. Like you have done so many times before.
>
> You are no stranger to upheaval. The problems of the past have made you stronger than most. You can be bent but nothing can crumble you. Like a fighter in the ring,

you have been knocked out. You may be down but not out. Definitely not out.

I meant it when I told you that if you want to grieve and heal quietly, you are welcome to come here to Las Vegas. You can be yourself and would not have to do anything that you don't want to. We have an extra room and you can stay there, under the covers all day if you so desire. Solitude can be very therapeutic. And if you want to talk, you have both of us.

Just think about this and there is no formality at all. If your presence is needed in India and you need to stay close to home and work, we completely understand. But if you think a change might be welcome, there is no better place than lovely Las Vegas. I will drive you to Grand Canyon and we can see the sunrise like you have never seen before. Or I can take you to the Pacific to show you how calm the deepest ocean in the world can be. Or we can just stay home, and I will cook the most delicious vegetarian meals you have tasted.

So, my dear darling child, think about it.

With love as always,
Uncle Kannan

Hello my dear Nandini,

Reading your email, I am infused with pride. You are being put through the test of fire and you are coming through with determination and courage. One can never suffer the loss you did and be 'normal' again.

Normal is hardly what others say it is. You have now got to learn the meaning of a sea-change in your life. If possible, try to re-invigorate the good memories of the life you had with Murali. I remember once being told that people that we love are only on loan to us and when it is re-paid, they are gone—forever. You are indeed correct in saying that you are re-building your life step by step.

It is likely that so many triggers on a day to day basis can push you off the tightrope that you are walking. A picture here, a piece of clothing there, a letter here or a memento there can open the flood gates and the feeling of loss gushes through, ready to drown you. Be sure to hold on to the raft of realisation that you are here and he is not. Murali loved you with all that he could and would not want to see you fall prey to a tidal wave of sorrow. There is no playbook to deal with loss such as yours.

Given your gift for writing, perhaps you should put down on paper how you are coping. You are starting a new chapter in your book of life. You are chartering untested waters. Writing your thoughts might give you a perspective on the life that was and the one that will be.

You are young, creative and vibrant. You have always searched for answers where others have failed to look. Perhaps something that can come out of this misery, the proverbial silver lining, might be a self-help book for others who have lost a loved one. Whether it is a man or a woman, the deeply wounded heart responds the same way. There are folks out there, trapped in expectations of others as to how they should respond to grief.

You might be a beacon to get them to cross that bridge of sorrow without fearing the water that is roaring underneath. There is life waiting after the crossing. Your life has not ended with his. He had to do what he had to do. But you have to now pick up the pieces. Anger and resentment are normal. They are the double-humped camels that you will have to ride to traverse this desert to reach the oasis of the future.

And what is that oasis? Peace of mind? Contentment with work? Excelling in a career that is yours for the taking? Helping others who are less fortunate? Showing 'the world that the 'us' has become 'me'? Slowly moving to a future that may direct you to a different life? A life that takes you on a road less travelled?

I don't know. But this I know. You are unsinkable. And you will be drawn by the right magnet to pull you out of the abyss. Remember that the unconventional woman in you needs to comfort and repair the conventional woman in you. I do not have to tell you that there are several alters in all of us. You need to draw on the strong ones in you to help the weaker ones.

With love as always,
Uncle Kannan

Unknown to my uncle, his letters to me became the inspiration for much of what I did later, including the writing of this book.

According to the World Health Organization (WHO), globally, 800,000 people die by suicide every year. Every 40 seconds, someone in the world dies by suicide. Every 40 seconds, a family is left to make sense of it.

Like me. Millions like me. Suicide is not the loss of just one precious life. According to the American Association of Suicidology, every completed suicide leaves six people bereaved.

Like a powerful earthquake, it throttles and dislodges the very foundation of our lives, causes irreparable fault lines. As we, survivors of suicide loss, survey the wreckage of our lives, we stoop to pick up fragments in the debris, yearning for a glimpse of stability—for life to become 'normal'. But the harsh reality is that life will never be 'normal' for us again. The old, the familiar and the known have all been reduced to rubble.

I certainly do not wish to paint a dystopian picture. One of the most influential writers I discovered at this point in my grief journey was Alan Wolfelt, a well-known grief counsellor, author and educator. When someone we love dies by suicide, the fabric of our lives ruptures at the seams. According to Wolfelt, to be 'bereaved' literally means 'to be torn apart'. Contrary to popular stereotypes that one needs to 'conquer' grief or 'subdue' and 'tame', Wolfelt suggests that we honour and embrace grief because it 'is life-sustaining and life-giving'.

Currently, we live in a culture that has no language to engage imaginatively with the pain of bereavement. We are taught to ignore, deny or get over it. We pathologise the very natural process of coming to terms with the inevitability of pain.

In the course of my grief journey, I gained insights into grieving and mourning. Thomas Attig, in his remarkable book *How We Grieve: Relearning the World* differentiates between grief and grieving. The former, he says, is a constellation of emotions we experience when we lose someone dear to us. It is part of the bereavement process. We have no choice when it comes to the bereavement: it is 'choiceless'. What we do have is a choice in how we respond to it.

According to Attig, grieving is a coping process in which we gradually adjust or recalibrate our lives to the reality of the loss. In other words, we relearn how to relate to the world. The relearning is not primarily cognitive and includes the emotional or affective components.

'Relearning the world is a multi-dimensional process, a multifaceted transitional process of learning *how* to live meaningfully after the loss. To be sure, this relearning is partly cognitive, but that is by no means the whole or the most important part,' writes Attig.

After Murali's death, there were multiple losses I had to confront. The death of my partner was undoubtedly the primary loss. But there were also several other invisible, intangible or secondary losses, which manifested themselves in different ways. I felt as though a large part of me was missing. It had gone with Murali. My role as a wife was non-existent. My status in society as the wife of a well-known doctor was erased. On the professional front, inspired by feminist values, Murali was never my calling card—in fact, most people discovered only much later that I was his wife.

I had to contend with the loss of routine. I am an excellent cook, and Murali was a connoisseur of food. After his death, I did not step into the kitchen. The memory of the last meal I cooked for him and his response to it still lingers in my mind. For nearly a year, I froze when I stepped into the kitchen. The loss of our shared life was devastating. As someone who had no idea of finance, I felt overwhelmed by being solely responsible for myself. At fifty-four, I found myself at a crossroads, alone.

Until Murali's death, I had been dismissive of mourning rituals. Rather self-opinionated and completely oblivious of the dharmic traditions that are my Hindu heritage, I trashed them as superfluous. However, the tragedy changed my perspective. Mourning, I discovered, is the outward expression of grief. People in India are vocal and expressive in their mourning. They cry, shout, scream and express their sorrow using evocative language, both verbal and non-verbal. Women, used to being more expressive, tend to be more vocal in their mourning. In some parts of India, such as southern Tamil Nadu and Rajasthan, we have professional mourners who are an integral part of mourning in any house where a death has occurred. In contrast to the 'stiff upper-lip' cultures that value restraint and reticence, mourning in India has been community-centric and collective. However, like the fate of many other time-honoured practices, the winds of modernity have begun to erode this bastion of tradition too.

In the Hindu Brahmin tradition, for instance, we perform monthly ceremonies for a one-year period after the death of a person. To my own surprise, I began to perform them religiously every month, preferring this to the other option presented to me—one where the ceremonies can be grouped and performed at one go. Every ceremony was either preceded or followed by an intense grief reaction that completely shook me. Strangely, it was cathartic and healing. I plumbed the depths of my sorrow, touched rock bottom and surfaced. Each time I re-emerged, I sloughed off layers of grief. I was torn, lacerated by the wild, jagged edges of sorrow. Yet, in my pain lay my healing and transformation, as over the next one year, I reclaimed myself from the ravages of pain and sorrow. This period marked by the grief rituals is a rite of passage both for the departed *atma* and the people left behind. It was a period when I truly relearnt the world.

My parents and I also performed special rites for Murali's *atma* at Rameswaram. This ritual, known as *atma visarjanam*, or releasing the *atma*, is a shastric practice involving elaborate pooja rituals, wherein the *atma* is helped to ascend as part of its onward journey. I performed this ritual on the seashore in Rameswaram, expertly guided by a senior priest from the temple town. A silver form (symbolic of the deceased person) was specially made and consecrated in pooja for ten days. At the end of a three-hour ceremony, when the priest instructed me to fling the form into the sea, I clung to it. I felt like I was holding on to Murali for a last few precious seconds.

As the waves washed it away to eternity, I prayed for Murali's *atma* to find eternal peace—a peace that had eluded him in his earthly life. He was a well-known urologist. Brilliant, bright and bold, he had studied at some of the most prestigious medical colleges in the country—the All India Institute of Medical Sciences, Maulana Azad Medical College, and Jawaharlal Institute of Postgraduate Medical Education and Research. Regarded as one of the finest urologists in the country, his expertise in andrology, paediatric urology and renal transplantation (of which he had successfully performed more than 1,500) was legendary. He was unanimously acknowledged by his peers and students as a 'phenomenal clinician and a gifted surgeon'. And yet, he had chosen to leave it all behind.

The five primal elements were witness to my final act of letting go. Murali was now an invisible, indivisible part of the grandeur of the cosmos.

Three months after Murali's death, I slept deeply and peacefully through the night for the first time. When I woke up the next morning, I experienced a deep sense of stillness—I was a new person, just born, forged in the crucible of tragedy.

PART II

Connecting with Carla

There are some things you can only learn in a storm.
—Anonymous

Like Tom Hanks's character Chuck Noland in the film *Castaway*, who found his lifeline in a volleyball which he named Wilson, I was helped by serendipity. My lifeline was two books—*No Time to Say Goodbye: Surviving the Suicide of a Loved One* by Carla Fine and *Touched by Suicide: Hope and Healing after Loss* by Michael F. Myers and Carla Fine. They found me when I was shipwrecked by grief, became beacons that guided my voyage across an uncharted ocean and anchored me during the year that I spent reconstructing my life, one moment at a time.

I found that there were several commonalities I shared with Carla. The most obvious was that Carla's husband, Harry Reiss, had been a well-known urologist with a successful practice in New York. Like me, Carla was the one to discover that her husband had died by suicide. Her book helped me understand the many complex and complicated aspects of grief associated with suicide loss. I also realised that, despite the differences in culture, as survivors of suicide loss, there were more similarities in our situations and responses than differences.

'In my mourning, I too wanted to be like everyone else. I wanted my family and friends to comfort me, not to question me why Harry had killed himself. I wanted to grieve my husband's absence, not analyse the reasons for his dying. I wanted to celebrate his kindness and friendship throughout the twenty-one years of our marriage, not to rage at him for abandoning me in the prime of our lives,' writes Carla.[1]

I read the book in one long stretch from start to finish. Carla was the first survivor of suicide loss I met—first through her book and later in person. Even reading the book felt like an intimate conversation with someone who had actually lived through the pain and anguish of suicide bereavement. From the initial impact of the suicide, through the messy aftermath, to reinventing myself and my life, Carla was my inspiration.

For the first time, I felt unburdened of the need to provide long explanations for why I felt the way I did. For many, I was an object of voyeurism and speculation. I lived my private grief in the fishbowl of public gaze and scrutiny, coloured by the lens of judgement.

Take, for instance, the immediate aftermath of the suicide, when the police came home. I immediately felt like the prime accused: my home resembled a crime scene with swarms of police personnel and visitors who had turned into inquisitive onlookers. It was impossible to share my experience with others. I felt as though we lacked a common language, syntax, grammar and vocabulary. In desperation, I tried to shield myself from everyone. The pall of shame was tangible, as was my naked vulnerability in the glare of judgement, blame and silent accusation.

When Carla described her own experiences, they resonated deeply with me. For the first time, I felt heard, seen and acknowledged. I felt validated. I understood how the standard procedure of treating every fatal suicide as a murder, until proven otherwise, is a harrowing experience for survivors of suicide loss across the globe, and that this exacerbates our primary loss and causes secondary victimisation.

---

[1] Carla's quotes in this chapter are both from her books and her correspondence with me.

'The fact that suicide is considered a criminal act comes as an abrupt shock to most survivors. Even as we are trying to absorb the unexpected and often violent deaths of our loved ones, we find ourselves dealing with the intricacies of a law enforcement system that is largely unfamiliar and somewhat threatening to us. If we are lucky, the police is sensitive; if we are confronted with hostile accusations, our self-ordained role as an accomplice to a murder is confirmed and validated,' she writes.

I emailed Carla immediately after finishing her book, not expecting her to reply. I thanked her for her incredible courage in sharing her journey as a survivor of suicide loss. I told her that her indomitable will, courage and resilience had become my strength and inspiration. To my delight, she responded almost instantly.

> Dear Nandini, I am so sorry about the suicide of your husband and am amazed about the coincidences of our experiences. Thank you so much for reaching out to me and I hope my book offered you some comfort during these crazy and awful times …
>
> From one survivor to another,
> Carla

Over the months, Carla and I stayed in touch.

From the very beginning of my grief voyage, although rudderless and adrift, I was determined to stay afloat. I was certain that I did not want to drown, and even while I was grasping at straws, my intent was clear—to emerge from the tragedy. I strongly believe that we manifest our intentions.

Carla, much like her book, became one of my lifelines. She helped reframe and recast a horrific event into an empowering narrative so I could rewrite the story of my life. I learnt that Carla was tempted to cover up her husband's suicide just like I had been. There was pressure from Murali's family to 'hush up' the cause of the death. One part of me felt acutely embarrassed about the suicide.

Do I tell it as it was or make up socially acceptable reasons—this was an ever-present dilemma. But Carla's perspective on the issue helped me through.

'My initial reaction was also to cover up Harry's suicide. I told everyone except for a few close friends and my immediate family that Harry had suffered a heart attack. I don't know who I was protecting—Harry or myself. Now I think I was protecting both of us: I didn't want people to think Harry was "disturbed" in any way nor did I want to be blamed for being a "bad" wife who couldn't even keep her husband alive. It takes a lot of work to keep up a lie and I found avoiding the truth to be draining and exhausting.'

Carla's quest for authenticity struck a chord with me. However, the real test came a few days after Murali's death, when I met a friend at the airport who breezily enquired, 'How's Murali?'

I paused for a microsecond. 'He's dead,' I blurted, dreading the next question.

'How?'

'Suicide.'

I heard the words loud and clear for the first time. My friend, thankfully, did not badger me with 'Why?'

I cannot pretend that my decision to speak the truth was consequence-free. As death by suicide is not a 'conventional' death, people were, and are, often flummoxed by my response. They don't know how or what to say. The knee-jerk response would be to perhaps blame me for having caused it or failed to prevent it.

However, that honest encounter at the airport made me stronger and gave me the conviction to speak my truth. In retrospect, my decision to 'come out' of the suicide closet was about my journey towards authenticity. I decided it was time to peel away the layers of masks I was hiding behind. All along, I was in touch with the feelings that were bubbling inside me. I managed them by consciously engaging in self-compassion and self-love. However, that all-important first step gave me the courage to own my story and share whatever felt right for me, and I must credit Carla for this.

'As I reluctantly began to accept Harry's decision—with heartache and regret—I started telling the truth when and if I cared to. I also began to understand that privacy is different from secrecy, and it's your story to tell or not tell as you see fit,' she writes in her book. These have become words I live by.

When I visited New York in 2018, I met with Carla. It's not often that one gets to meet a prolific author—especially not one with a master's in journalism from the prestigious Columbia School of Journalism and author of several books. Carla's father, Benjamin Fine, was the education editor of *The New York Times*. Carla also has an abiding Indian connection: her late sister Janet Fine lived in Bombay for most of her life.

I spent a wonderful evening with Carla, her husband Allan and their two adorable dogs, Jancy and Benji, walking around Chelsea. It was capped off by an amazing dinner at an Italian vegan restaurant. Carla and I share a sisterhood, and I am touched that she now considers me her 'Indian sister'.

As she writes in her book, 'Suicide is incredibly humbling. It makes you realise that no matter how much you love or care for other people, you cannot be their life support system, you cannot keep them going, you can't will your spirit over to them. Our loved one's death by suicide is not our choice, yet we who are left behind, must learn to live with its consequences and deal with its aftermath.'

I, too, realised that I had to abdicate responsibility for Murali's suicide. People are responsible for their own actions, not the actions of those around them. However, I came to realise that this is not something most survivors of suicide loss have internalised. When I meet them, I witness their inflated sense of responsibility that morphs into self-blame for having failed to prevent the suicide of their loved ones.

My own healing began the moment I realised that I had nothing to do with Murali's decision to take his life. I realised that in order to heal completely, I had to stop questioning or judging him for it. He had chalked out a dysfunctional strategy to deal with his pain, and when I put myself in his place, I wonder if I would have done the same thing had I been in the kind of pain he was in.

'Even though suicide is not our decision, our lives are irreversibly altered by its consequences. Harry did not ask either for my permission or my blessing. In order to forgive not only him but also myself, I had to accept that, ultimately, it was Harry's own choice to kill himself. All I can do is disagree with his decision,' writes Carla. Her book was the gateway to a host of other books on surviving suicide loss, most of them written by survivors. I was pleasantly surprised by all the literature available to me, but was struck by the lack of books like Carla's in the Indian context.

Why was it not possible to tell our stories in India? What was holding us back? Would we rather gloss over, not talk about it or 'hush up the death' as one close family member had urged me to do? How many suicides does it take before we decide to speak up, before we realise that preventing suicide is everybody's business?

The 4S's: Stigma, Shame, Secrecy and Silence

> Shame is a soul-eating emotion.
> —Carl Jung

A few years ago, I met a woman whose husband had died by suicide many years back. We were participants in an experiential inner healing workshop, and each of us was processing grief, anger, resentment, fear and other toxic emotions. This woman was still angry with her husband for 'abandoning' the family. When I joined the suicide loss club, I decided that I needed to experience my anger fully and transform it into something more affirming. I certainly did not want to hold on to my anger and resentment for a lifetime.

When confronted with Murali's suicide, I too had been overcome by a sense of shame and guilt. Shame implies a sense of 'I am bad', while guilt implies that 'I have done something bad'. In both instances, I was caught up in thinking about what I would tell my family and friends.

How did I 'catch' it? There is no immunity—at least in the early phase of suicide bereavement—to the viral load of the 4S's. Dominant narratives of suicide locate it in the context of crime and sin. It is viewed through the lens of morality and perceived as a character flaw: religion conflates it with sin, while the law equates it with crime. The media sensationalises it and either glorifies or demonises the victim. This is exemplified in the language that dominates suicide narratives. We say that people who have died by suicide have 'committed' suicide, which implies that suicide is a crime and equates it with self-murder. Such insensitive and non-critical language reinforces the mainstream view of suicide as a crime.

A stigma is a mark of disgrace. It is something to be ashamed of and is located within a larger social context that tends to view a particular issue, and the people impacted by it, in a negative light. It is often fuelled by ignorance, prejudice, rigidity and judgement. Mental illness, suicide and HIV/AIDS are highly stigmatised, for example. While the first two are perceived as character flaws or moral failings, HIV/AIDS is additionally associated with taboos around sex and sexuality, in a clear case of social stigma.

Suicide is mired in stigma, myths and misconceptions despite the fact that it is a great leveller and nobody is immune to it. Suicidologists agree that every human being has two strong impulses embedded within themselves: Eros, the life-affirming impulse, and Thanatos, the life-denying impulse. For many, Eros dominates, and as a result, they embrace life. On the other hand, when Thanatos dominates, people are driven to kill themselves. Of course, these impulses need to be viewed in a larger framework of risk factors that increase the likelihood of suicide and protective factors that prevent it.

'Suicide breaks all the rules. People we know and hold dear have defied the course of nature and determined when and how they died. Our loved one's act throws our own perceptions to the winds, our way of looking at life and death is sundered. The question, "Why do we die?" has always been an unanswerable mystery; with suicide, the question reshapes into, "Why did my loved one choose to die?"' writes Carla.

Social stigma perpetuates negative attitudes and stereotypes about suicide that people almost always internalise. As a result of this skewed perspective, we tend to judge the act of suicide, as well as those who died by suicide, suicide-attempt survivors and survivors of suicide loss. I judged Murali too: I was enraged that he had wilfully abandoned me. I felt rejected. 'Even my love was not enough for you!' I screamed as I pummelled my pillow with pent-up force each night.

It is important to note that people impacted by suicide tend to internalise feelings of shame, blame and judgement. For almost a year after my husband's suicide, I grappled with two core survivor questions: Why didn't I anticipate it and take preventive measures? Was there anything I could have done to prevent it? It is this corrosive self-stigma that make suicide bereavement qualitatively different from normative bereavement.

When I experienced rage—directed at both Murali and myself—I thought it was unique to survivors of suicide loss. But now, I am aware that even if Murali had died of natural causes, I would have been angry. After all, anger is the first stage of the grief cycle in the Kubler–Ross model—I would have been angry at life and fate. But it may have been unalloyed anger, devoid of the toxic emotions of guilt, self-blame and self-reproach. The writer Maggie White sums up the symbiosis between shame and stigma thus: 'Self-stigma is the birthplace of shame. And shame and stigma have been doing a destructive, cyclical dance for long.'[1]

It is common for people to blame the victim or their family, not realising that there are multiple forces that drive a person to suicide, and as White writes, 'lie with the forces of suicide itself in the same way that people die of other illnesses'. We wouldn't blame a person or their family when the cause of death is non-suicidal, so why do we indulge in blame games and accusations when it comes to suicide? People asked me flippant questions when they came to offer their condolences: 'Didn't you see it coming?' 'Were there any clues?' 'If you had been there and not travelling, could you have averted it?'

---

[1] http://www.oursideofsuicide.com/2015/05/28/shame-stigma-mental-illness/.

Negative attitudes can be conveyed through a network of intertwined pathways: gossip, relentless speculation, intrusive probing, negative media portrayals, insensitivity, social isolation, naming and blaming of suicide victims and their families. Or worse, there is the wall of silence that makes it clear that suicide is a social and cultural taboo and, therefore, not to be talked about openly. This seems to be the universal experience of survivors of suicide loss across cultures, especially when they happen to be women.

Take the case of Reena, a twenty-year-old undergraduate student in Madurai who had a loving relationship with her father, who she says was a nurturing, caring and doting parent. She was closer to her father than to her mother. People in their small community knew about the bond she shared with him. However, when Reena's father died by suicide, the needle of suspicion swung towards her. 'I was shocked to hear of my father's suicide. He seemed so normal that day when he sent me off to college. Immediately, people pounced on my mother and began to pester her about the cause of the suicide. They were unable to find a convincing answer. However, they spread rumours about my involvement with a boy and insinuated that fearing a scandal, my father had killed himself. From that day onwards, until today, my mobility is being policed by the women in the neighbourhood,' recalls Reena, who admits that her brother was never the object of such blaming, shaming and speculation.

I agree with Reena when she says that had her father died of other causes, she would not have been targeted by the community. Such speculations adversely impact and exacerbate the trauma of survivors of suicide loss. They compound one's primary loss and grief. The social stigma of suicide leads to self-stigma that is associated with low self-worth, guilt, shame and self-blame, which influence our grief trajectories and well-being.

If a parent loses a child to suicide, the trajectory is similar, yet unique in its own way. A child's suicide reverses the normative order of life that parents precede their children in death. Parents who survive the suicide of their son or daughter are often blamed for having failed in their parental duty of 'protecting' their children.

Take, for instance, Meenakshi Raja and S. Raja, a soft-spoken and erudite couple who teach at a college in Karaikudi, a town near Madurai. Theirs was a stereotypically happy family, with parents providing tender, loving support to their two brilliant sons. The family was close knit and spent a lot of time together—at dinner, over the weekends and travelling whenever possible. Bhuvanesh, the younger boy, was a class twelve student. He had been a topper throughout his life, scoring a GPA of 4.8/5 in class ten. With the board examination just a few months away, his teachers expected him to surpass this performance.

According to his parents, teachers and family, Bhuvanesh was an affectionate, caring and fun-loving boy, and everybody's favourite. He was adored by his teachers and peers. One day, when his parents returned from work, they found that their son had hanged himself. 'People were quick to point fingers at us. Our parenting style was questioned. We were accused of having failed to prevent the suicide. Our son's teachers, classmates and parents refused to have anything to do with us. In the early days, I felt comforted if I talked to my son's classmates and often phoned them up. They responded a couple of times, and then they refused to take my calls. I suppose their parents would have warned them to distance themselves,' recalls Meenakshi Raja.

Her husband admits that the negative media publicity mentioned the victim's name and school. These additional factors exacerbate the primary loss in suicide bereavement and make grieving a slow, agonising and isolating experience for survivors. Interestingly, such accusations need not be explicit. Often, they are subtle and subversive, and as survivors of suicide loss, we are acutely sensitive and perceptive to such sub-texts.

No one pointed fingers at me blatantly for Murali's suicide, especially when it became known that he had been struggling with bipolar depression for years. Yet, I picked up the silent accusations. The verdict: In a conventional sense, despite everything, the suicide sealed my performance appraisal as a wife; I had failed. My childfree status bolstered my inadequacy as a woman—I was a 'childless' widow, a typical patriarchal label.

Sigmund Freud made a pertinent observation that seems as valid today as it was decades ago. Commenting on a friend who died by suicide, he said, 'What drove him to it? As an explanation, the world is ready to hurl the ghastliest accusations at the unfortunate widow.'

By internalising and amplifying the blame attributed to them, survivors of suicide loss become their own worst enemies. I often wondered if I should have acted on my impulse to ring Murali on the night he decided to end his life. There was nothing specific I had to share with him, and since I would be meeting him in the morning, I had postponed the call. Could my call have made the difference between life and death? Could it have tethered him to life? After all, that night, around the presumed time of Murali's death, I had experienced a great sense of unease and discomfort. Even months after the incident, I reconstructed his last moments in my mind in a desperate attempt to make sense of it all. Should I have listened to my inner voice when I sensed that there was something unusual in the parting gift that Murali had given me? I constantly wrestle with the 'would have/could have/should have' interrogative process, relentlessly post-morteming my lack of prescience.

I indulged in this self-flagellation despite the fact that I had done everything a human being could possibly do for another. However, the reality of suicide—the shock and the traumatic impact—leaves one gasping like a fish out of water. We asphyxiate on our own toxic emotions of guilt and shame. 'The decision to die of suicide creates a sense of utter helplessness for those of us who are left behind. In order to maintain a sense of control, we often blame the deaths of our loved ones on actions we took or omissions we made,' writes Carla, in the book that eventually became my guiding light, *No Time to Say Goodbye*.

When I met Carla, we spoke about the ramifications of blame and self-blame for survivors. Following her husband's death, Carla recalled that she had faulted everyone she knew—his friends, family and colleagues—for not standing by her husband. 'Most of all, I blamed myself. It seemed inconceivable that my life force had not been strong enough to keep both of us alive,' she said.

Like a festering mould, the stigma around suicide proliferates in the darkness of ignorance, fear and negative stereotypes. In his book *Getting Grief Right: Finding Your Story of Love in the Sorrow of Loss*, co-author Patrick O'Mallery, a well-known grief psychotherapist, talks about the intergenerational impact of stashing away a suicide in the family as a closely guarded secret.

O'Mallery's paternal grandmother died by suicide when his father was ten years old. Her husband told their son that she had died of pneumonia. But, even as a young boy, O'Mallery's father sensed that the cause of death was something 'different'. Just a few hours before she killed herself, his mother had tripped on one of his toys. For many years, O'Mallery's father blamed himself for his mother's death because he had left his toys sprawled on the floor.

'What he did not know, he attempted to imagine, an example of the need to create stories so that we can try to make sense of our world. My father was haunted by the story he created,' writes O'Mallery.

O'Mallery's father shared this story with him when he was twenty years old. Several years later, his father tracked down the doctor who had falsely certified the cause of his mother's death. The doctor confessed that he had 'covered up the suicide' and passed it off as death due to natural causes because of pressure from O'Mallery's grandfather, who was also a doctor and his colleague. O'Mallery's father had finally discovered the truth, and it set him free. He learnt that his mother's death had nothing to do with his toys. The truth released him from self-blame; he had redeemed himself in his own eyes. He also learnt that the conspiracy of silence was a conscious choice of secrecy over public shame and disgrace. At the time of his mother's suicide, the act was considered a mortal sin by the Catholic church, and suicide victims were denied burial in a Catholic cemetery.

'When he came home from that trip, my dad seemed like a different man. A weight that he had carried since he was ten years old was finally gone. He had lived with guilt and confusion for a lifetime because of the secret that was kept and a story that was never told. Once he knew the true story, he could step out from the shadow where he lived and be more present to his life,' writes O'Mallery.

By now, I was in sight of a nebulous roadmap with which to navigate the wilderness of suicide grief. It would be a lonely and desolate journey, I knew. Although I had no strategic plan, I felt compelled to be the change I wished to see. I wanted to reform the narrative of suicide from blame and judgement to one of compassion and empathy that would create safe, supportive spaces for conversations on suicide. But for that to happen, I had to detangle the warp and weft of stigma, shame, secrecy and silence that threatened to insidiously weave themselves into the tapestry of my life.

Owning Our Stories

Choosing authenticity is not an easy choice. To be nobody but yourself in a world which is doing its best, night and day, to make you everybody but yourself—means to fight the hardest battle which any human being can fight and never stop fighting. 'Staying real' is one of the most courageous battles that we'll ever fight.

—E.E. Cummings

I realised early on that it was important for me to own my story and to tell it as is. To my advantage, I simultaneously realised that shame would be a disempowering emotion with which I would have to contend. I was ready for the challenge. The desire to be authentic—to be my real self and not what others expected me to be—outweighed my desire to achieve a false sense of safety and be deceptively anchored in the quicksand of my comfort zone.

'If we want to live and love with our whole heart, and if we want to engage with the world from a place of worthiness, we have to talk about the things that get in the way—especially shame, fear and vulnerability,' writes Brené Brown, professor of Social Work, in her book *The Gifts of Imperfection: Let Go of Who You Think You're Supposed to Be and Embrace Who You Are*.

Shame is a universal emotion. All of us experience shame at some point in our lives. However, in the context of suicide loss, shame acquires unexplored dimensions and implications. When Carl Jung famously described shame as a 'soul-eating emotion', he was referring to its disempowering nature. A person experiencing shame will downsize and altogether deny the reality of their experience by disowning their stories, for shame makes one feel small, flawed and unworthy.

Jungian analysts describe shame as the 'swampland of the soul'. Developing the metaphor, Brown writes, 'We need to learn how to wade through it. We need to see that standing on the shore and catastrophising about what could happen if we talked honestly about our fears is actually more painful than grabbing the hand of a trusted companion and crossing the swamp. And most important, we need to learn why constantly trying to maintain our footing on the shifting shore as we gaze across the other side of the swamp—where our worthiness waits for us—is much harder work than trudging across.'

This has profound implications for people who have survived suicide loss. We are compelled to hide our truths because we are afraid that people will reject us, judge us and blame us. We are afraid of being perceived as unworthy of love and belonging. Worse, we are afraid that the suicide of a loved one will define our reality and circumscribe us.

I chose to acknowledge, understand and honour my shame, which resulted in a reduction of the guilt I was feeling. Choosing to tell my truth was an act of courage that neutralised shame because shame cannot fester under the light of awareness.

One day, I came across the term 'shame resilience', which validated my stance and my experiences. Developed by Brown in 2006, shame resilience is a theory that defines shame, its consequences and how people respond to it. Shame causes people to feel 'trapped, isolated and useless', according to Brown. 'Shame resilience is the ability to recognise shame, move through it constructively while maintaining worthiness and authenticity, and to ultimately develop more courage, compassion and connection as a result of our experience. The first thing we need to understand about shame resilience is that the less we talk about shame, the more we have it.'

Shame resilience has important implications for those of us seeking to reconstruct our lives after suicide loss. We need to recognise and acknowledge the personal vulnerability that leads to the feeling of shame. In our vulnerability lies our strength. We also need to recognise the external factors. For example, suicide loss survivors have to recognise that the stigma, shame, secrecy and silence cause us to internalise these feelings and attitudes and indulge in self-blame.

We also need to connect with others to receive and offer empathy by telling our stories and making ourselves heard. Speaking about shame neutralises its power to harm us. It is also an effective protection against self-blame and self-abuse. We need to discuss and deconstruct the feelings of shame, both individually and collectively. Doing so lets people know that we would like them to support us and in what way. Often, people don't reach out because they don't know how to. We not only need to tell our stories truthfully, but also create spaces for supportive conversations that might enable survivors of suicide loss to speak up and those around them to offer support, while withholding blame and judgement.

Survivors of suicide loss need a sangha—a community of supportive people who can come together and create a sacred space. In doing so, we release shame and embrace self-worth, and forge forward with courage, compassion and conviction.

The 3C's: Courage, Compassion and Connection

> Only when we are brave enough to explore the darkness, will we discover the power of our light.
>
> —Brené Brown

Courage, compassion and connection are words that have enormous relevance in how we view suicide and issues related to it, particularly those around survivors of suicide loss. The Latin root of courage, *cor*, means heart. Originally, courage meant 'to speak one's mind by telling one's heart'.

It is interesting to note that the original sense of courage is still alive if we know where and how to look for it. From the perspective of survivors of suicide loss, courage means being open and accepting of one's vulnerabilities. It means encouraging other survivors of suicide loss to share their stories of vulnerabilities, to be seen and heard, acknowledged and validated.

Courage is a key factor in living in a space of authenticity, and I have discovered that authenticity is about choice. I made a conscious choice that I would be honest about the manner of Murali's death despite the pressure to cover it up. Hiding it was a game of endless deceptions for which I no longer had the bandwidth. Being honest, showing up and being real were important milestones in my journey towards authenticity. This audacity of authenticity enabled me to challenge the status quo by being subversive and transgressing the dominant narrative surrounding suicide loss in society. As Brown said, 'You have to be brave with your life so that others can be brave with theirs.'

Truly, being courageous about my lived experience of suicide loss has had a ripple effect. I once met a young man who was struggling with suicidal ideation. On hearing my story, he said to me, 'I want to live. If this is the impact suicide can have on those who are left behind, I don't want to subject my loved ones to this pain and anguish.'

In a traumatic bereavement like suicide, compassion is the salve for which one longs. Compassion, once again a word of Latin origin, means 'to suffer with'. Ironically, compassion is not our default setting. Whenever we see someone in pain, our first response is not to reach out to them but to self-protect. For example, a common response to a friend or relative losing a dear one to suicide is, 'I don't know what to tell him or her.' Our behaviour is marked by empathy deficit.

Human beings are hardwired for connection. It is in our biology. Right from the moment of birth, it is a vital force that helps us thrive physically, emotionally, socially and spiritually. Yet, when it comes to people and situations that don't fit society's definition of 'normal', we are conditioned to disconnect. This is evident in the world of suicide. Instead of developing a connection, we only foster isolation and exclusion by perpetuating negative stereotypes based on stigma and shame. However, if shame is the predominant disempowering emotion that shrouds suicide in a deafening silence and secrecy more impenetrable than the densest Amazonian rain forests, the three C's, courage, compassion and connection, can penetrate the darkest recesses of one's being.

For survivors of suicide loss and people who are supportive of them, here is my question: are we willing to tell our stories, listen to others' stories, genuinely feel their pain and stay connected with others in a world that is increasingly disconnected?

Making Meaning of Suicide Loss

> The quantity and quality of understanding support you get during your work of mourning will have a major influence on your capacity to heal. You cannot—nor should you try to—do this alone. Drawing on the experience and encouragement of friends and fellow grievers is not a weakness but a healthy human need.
>
> —Alan Wolfelt, *Understanding Your Grief*

Death by suicide is a mysterious, puzzling and confusing experience for the bereaved, compounded by the accompanying trauma. The grief following such a death (as with death by homicide, accident, and death due to natural disasters) is traumatic because of the violence of the act and its suddenness.

The suicide of my spouse was sudden and shocking. A violent death, it felt like an ambush. I was not only mourning the loss of a partner but also traumatised, even more so because I was the one who discovered the suicide.

Suicide is not an easy subject to talk about. It is commonly perceived as a private event motivated by dysfunctional individual behaviour and not a public health issue that impacts communities. Such negative stereotypes about suicide inform, influence and impact the trajectory of suicide grief, such that navigating grief becomes a lonely, isolating and frightening experience. Haunted by guilt, most survivors spend a disproportionate amount of time seeking to comprehend the motivations of the deceased.

'Standing under the mysterious experience of suicide grief provides us with a unique perspective. Maybe only after exhausting an instinctive search for the "why" of suicide can we discover a newly defined "why" for our lives,' writes Wolfelt in *Understanding Your Grief: Ten Essential Touchstones for Finding Hope and Healing Your Heart.*

In our desperate desire to make meaning, we are driven by an intense need to conduct a personal psychological autopsy. We try to make sense of the death and our role in the tragedy, with the limited pieces of the jigsaw puzzle, even as we desire to complete the big picture. It takes many agonising moments of truth to realise that no matter how hard we try, we may never know with certainty why our loved ones died the way they did. Healing begins with confronting and accepting this inconvenient truth.

'Suicide can shatter many of the things you take for granted about yourself, your relationships and your world,' writes John Jordan in *After Suicide Loss: Coping with Your Grief.* Among the many things that shatters is our perception of our loved one and the nature of our relationship with them. We are confronted with a harsh reality check: Did we really know our loved one at all? Or were we living with a stranger?

Survivors of suicide loss are confronted with several recurring impulses. First, we constantly feel the need to make meaning of this mysterious death. We try to decipher the motivations of the deceased, we explore our role in and responsibility for the death, and we are swamped by the resulting turbulent emotions of anger, guilt and blame—all of which are amplified and reinforced by the mainstream societal view of suicide as sin and crime.

'Suicide is a difficult conundrum,' writes Jordan. Unlike with other kinds of death, in suicide, the victim is also seen as the perpetrator. Naturally, survivors of suicide loss find themselves in a Catch-22 situation. I was angry with my husband for having rejected my love. His self-inflicted death felt like abandonment. I was also angry with myself for not having prevented such a tragedy.

Then there is the eternal question of the role of choice in suicide. Is suicide voluntary? An act of free will? Or is it influenced by psychological factors outside one's conscious control?

We are asked why our loved ones chose suicide because people are usually unaware that there is no simple, one-sentence explanation for it. A death by suicide disrupts social relationships. Most survivors of suicide loss are fearful and uncertain of how friends and family will view them. And most people, in turn, are equally uncertain and ignorant about how to respond appropriately to the bereaved. The latter fear discomfort; the former, condemnation and rejection. The ambiguity and ambivalence make bereavement profoundly isolating and alienating.

According to Jordan, a death by suicide also creates 'information management problems' in families. Most families agonise over how transparent they should be about divulging the cause of death. To tell or not to tell becomes a contentious issue that splits them. Most families, however, prefer to keep it secret—a decision that has a powerful impact on their eventual healing. As they struggle to create a shared narrative in the aftermath of the suicide, family discord and estrangement are secondary losses that a survivor of suicide loss may face. These compound and complicate the primary trauma and deprive survivors of valuable support in their transition journey.

Suicide shatters normative assumptions and stability in the survivor's world. Bereavement in this context has been rather evocatively described as 'grief with the volume turned on'. This simply means that emotions such as anger, fear, sadness and guilt that are common responses to loss are amplified and intensified. As a result, the grieving process is longer and more complex, aptly termed as complicated grief.

A death by suicide is fodder for wild speculation and gossip—it is a public death, and the medico-legal implications are many. Survivors, relatives and friends are unsure and confused, and are unable to come up with informed and sensitive responses. The stigma acts as a mirror, and as a result, survivors internalise the shame and negative societal attitudes towards it. They fear that they, and the victim, will be judged negatively, and end up isolating and withdrawing themselves. Such a loss of social networks and breakdown of interpersonal relationships, both within the family and outside, delays or stunts the healing of the survivors, who remain unheard and unseen.

It would be helpful if relatives and friends were sensitised to this issue, with consideration and thought given to compassionate ways of responding and making themselves present and available. This is a complicated matter that takes considerable effort to navigate, but doing so would provide much needed support to the survivor.

The complexity of suicide translates into the complexity of grief after a suicide death. During the early phase of my own bereavement, I felt as though no one understood my predicament. Naturally, how could they? Because suicide is a non-normative death, conventional yardsticks of grief and mourning cannot be automatically transposed. Despite their well-meaning intentions, I didn't think people understood. Worse, I sensed an empathy deficit in most people. They were too bewildered by the tragedy to display any meaningful empathy.

During my compulsive search for online resources on suicide bereavement, I discovered an online suicide bereavement support group called Grief Relief for Survivors of Suicide Loss. Impressed by their comprehensive ground rules—especially the one which stated that it was a closed group and membership was based on the lived experience of suicide loss—I stepped in tentatively. A peer-led initiative, the group is moderated and led by Linda Marshall Leroux, a survivor of suicide loss herself, grief psychotherapist and life coach.

For the first time, I ceased to feel alone. Meeting virtually with others who had been bereaved by suicide gave me hope and strength to move forward. Although there is no one approach to grief and grieving, knowing how others deal with their loss inspired and humbled me. I not only received but also offered unconditional support to others bereaved like me.

I felt a collective sense of support and empathy. All of us spoke the same language—we felt understood and heard. There were many others who, with grace, strength and endurance, had rebuilt their lives from the debris of unfathomable tragedy. Although it seemed like a mirage, it nevertheless sowed in me the seeds of possibility. Could I also rise above my own pain and reach out to others like me?

I am sometimes astonished by how far I have come in such a short time. More than a year after I lost Murali, I came across a post on the support group where one member detailed the pain of dealing with the first anniversary of her partner's suicide. I wrote, 'Thank you for your searing honesty and authenticity. Ever since I lost my husband to suicide, every day has been a challenge … Yes, the first year is incredibly challenging. I am told it takes at least three years to accommodate the loss into our lives. Meanwhile, we keep at it, keep moving on. We must learn not to push against the river but flow where it takes us.'

In another instance of serendipity, a couple who had lost their younger son to suicide discovered SPEAK—the suicide prevention initiative I set up in 2018—on the internet and reached out to me. That was also the beginning of the SPEAK Suicide Bereavement Support Group (SBSG). As the name implies, an SBSG is a forum or a platform for family members, friends, colleagues or mental health professionals who have lost loved ones to suicide.

The focus in these groups is on the survivors of suicide loss, not the victims. They focus on enabling members to build resilience in a safe, supportive and non-judgemental space. This allows members to process grief mindfully and develop a set of coping strategies that enables them to rebuild and transform their lives.

SBSGs can be online, offline or both, and they are either peer-led or moderated by mental health professionals. Personally, I find peer-led support groups more effective as there is no substitute for lived experience. Although each suicide is different and each affected person grieves differently, there is a unifying, unique bond in the group—the lived experience of traumatic grief.

These support groups provide us with the rare opportunity to explore this bond, interact with others and help each other heal. SBSGs counter isolation, restore people's trust and offer inspirational role models. Being non-hierarchical spaces, they consider everyone's experience equally valid, which means all the members are heard, seen and acknowledged.

The three core tasks of an SBSG are providing comfort (acknowledging the pain and being respectful of vulnerabilities), encouragement (normalising and validating the experience) and education (modelling healthy coping skills and strategies) for members. However, it is important to remember that an SBSG meeting is not a therapy or counselling session.

It is, rather, an important component in postvention services for survivors. The moderator usually encourages people to share their struggles with grief and their coping strategies, and the group offers the collective wisdom of access to resources, support and encouragement through shared experiences. The moderator needs to be particularly sensitive to the sharing of the manner of death as this could potentially be traumatising to others. In such instances, individual sharing, rather than in a group, is encouraged, followed by a referral to a grief counsellor or trauma therapist, if necessary.

Some of the common issues discussed during an SBSG meeting include myths and misconceptions about suicide; surviving suicide grief; coping with depression, anxiety, shame and guilt; children's grief; seeking professional support; building resilience and rebuilding one's life. There is no rule of thumb for when a bereaved person should join a support group. That said, a common sense approach would be to wait for at least a month after bereavement. Of course, the decision to seek support depends on the individual's choice. Families and friends could share with them the availability of such services.

Despite the innumerable benefits, initiating and sustaining an SBSG continues to be a huge challenge in Madurai, where I live. SPEAK initiated an offline support group for survivors of suicide loss, but after a few meetings, attendance dwindled. The stigma of suicide makes it difficult for survivors to come out and seek support. They are fearful of being seen in support groups because of the disapproval of family members. One person told me that their family would prefer they not talk about it as it would be a 'blot on the family name and honour'.

However, people who have a lived experience of suicide loss hold a mirror to each's other pain, helping to cope better and transition to a life without their loved one. Grieving and healing are both collective and individual. I am aware that among those who have been bereaved by suicide, there are similarities in experience, but these are rarely, if ever, identical. Yet, the similarities far outweigh the differences. When I meet people impacted by suicide loss, there is an instant kinship and connection. Such spaces, with bonds of compassion, care and concern, are the best antidote to the virus of stigma and shame.

Nevertheless, until we mainstream informed conversations about suicide that feature empathy and understanding, such initiatives will continue to have minimal impact. They may provide a desperately needed lifejacket to the drowning. But when one's vision in an ocean of grief is obscured by the stinging spray of stigma, shame, silence and secrecy, it is hard, even impossible, to see a rescue option, leave alone make use of it.

A Beautiful World

> If winter comes, can spring be far behind?
> —Percy Bysshe Shelley, 'Ode to the West Wind'

The picturesque city of Amsterdam in the Netherlands has played an important role in my grief journey. As one of twenty-five applicants chosen out of a pool of two hundred and fifty to attend the Professional Development Program in Gender conducted by the Royal Tropical Institute, I arrived in the city in October 2017. I spent the first day exploring the city. I visited the Van Gogh Museum, excited to see the paintings I had always been fascinated by. I was particularly struck by 'The Almond Tree in Bloom', which Vincent Van Gogh had painted to symbolise the dawn of spring in his life. Looking at it, I began to wonder if there would be spring in my life once again.

Six months later, when I returned to Amsterdam to complete the course, I knew that I had indeed travelled far in my journey and was approaching spring—I had performed Murali's first-year death ceremony and taken the flight out that same evening.

When I arrived in Amsterdam for the second time, it was spring in the European metropolis. The sun was lambent, gentle and soothing, and the cherry trees were in bloom. It was spring—a time of hope and new beginnings—in my life too. I completed the course and was commended by the directors, Maitrayee Mukhopadhyay and Franz Wong, both fine professionals and even finer human beings. It was a moment of great personal pride and satisfaction.

Amsterdam will forever be special for me. During the one week I spent there, I wandered the streets, sat by the sparkling canal and got lost in reflections of the year that had gone by. I spent time connecting with myself and was reminded that despite life's trials, it is important to remember that we live in a beautiful world.

When life throws challenges at you, it also sends you people who seem to appear out of nowhere. One such person in my life is Maitrayee. She made it possible for me to complete the course by giving me an extra three days (which I had missed due to Murali's ceremony) and personally took me through the course syllabus. I will forever cherish her sisterhood, the warmth of her friendship and the grace of her presence.

Thank you, Amsterdam, for restoring a sense of perspective in my life and for helping me come full circle. Despite life's challenges, trials and struggles, it still is a beautiful world!

From Pain to Purpose

> Pain is the hammer of the gods to break
> A dead resistance in the mortal's heart
> —Sri Aurobindo, *Savitri: A Legend and a Symbol*

Margaret Mitchell, the well-known American author said, 'Life is under no obligation to give us what we expect.'

I've got nothing I *wanted* from life, but I am grateful it has given me everything I *need*. I have faced many challenges, with suicide loss being the most profound. In retrospect, I have realised that embedded in each of these challenges was an opportunity to grow and become the best possible version of myself.

The statistics are grim.

- Every 40 seconds, someone in the world dies by suicide.
- Every 41 seconds, someone is bereaved by suicide loss.
- For every person who dies by suicide, 25 people attempt it.
- Across the world, 800,000 people die by suicide every year.
- Globally, suicide is the second-leading cause of death among 15 to 29-year-olds.
- India accounts for 17 per cent of the world's suicides.
- Every year, 136,000 people in India die by suicide.
- In India, a person dies by suicide every 4 minutes.
- Between 2002 and 2012, the suicide rate in the country increased by 22.7 per cent.
- India has the highest suicide rate in the world among the 15 to 29 age group.

- The Indian states of Maharashtra, Tamil Nadu and West Bengal account for the maximum number of suicides in the country.
- Among the 53 mega-cities in India, Chennai (2,274), Bengaluru (1,885), Delhi (1,553) and Mumbai (1,122) together have reported almost 34.6 per cent of total suicides in Indian cities.
- India accounts for 40 per cent of the world's suicides among women.

Source: WHO (2017-19), Lancet Public Health 2017 and National Crime Records Bureau (NCRB)

What do these statistics mean? People who die by suicide are not mere numbers. They convey the sheer prevalence of suicide, show us that there is at least one person in our social circle who has attempted or is thinking about suicide. In spite of these facts, we choose to look away. We do not see suicide as a threat until someone important to us dies by it. Until then, it remains as something that would never happen to us or to our family.

The very subject of suicide catches everybody's attention. But sadly, the actions that lead up to it go unnoticed. Suicide has long been associated with extreme emotions: fear, cowardice, shame, sin, crime and even heroism. However, rather than treating it from a public health perspective and acknowledging its prevalence, we treat it as a rare and distant incident.

In order to break the silence around suicide, we need to better understand what exactly goes through the mind of someone thinking about it. We also have to consider survivors of suicide loss and the issues they face because of the lack of support and care. Such informed perspectives are important to create safe, supportive spaces for conversations on suicide.

The term suicide is derived from the Latin phrase *sui caedere*, which means 'to kill oneself'. According to the American Association of Suicidology, 'the primary goal of suicide is not to end life; but to end pain'. People who die by suicide choose death over living because their 'psyche ache' is unbearable—it is so intense that death seems to be a preferable alternative.

Suicide is an issue that has plagued societies around the world for many years. And it has almost always been viewed through the lens of morality. This is largely a legacy of religion; most major religions say that the right to take one's life is not a human prerogative. Legal jurisprudence incorporated this moral perspective into laws that regard taking one's life as a criminal act and therefore punishable.

Currently, however, fifty-nine countries, including India, have decriminalised attempted suicide. This includes the whole of Europe, North America, much of South America and parts of South Asia. In north European countries such as Denmark, Norway and Sweden, this came into effect in the early nineteenth century.

England, which bequeathed its legal legacy to independent India, decriminalised suicide way back in 1961. But, until recently, based on Section 309 of the Indian Penal Code, attempted suicide was considered a crime in India and punishable by imprisonment for a year and/or imposition of a fine. Although the Delhi High Court observed in 1985 that 'The continuance of Section 309 is an anachronism unworthy of a human society like ours,' attempted suicide continued to be treated as a crime.

Finally, thanks to consistent advocacy by mental health activists, the Mental Health Care Act passed in the Indian parliament in 2017 decriminalised suicide. Even though Section 309 has not yet been struck down, this act considerably reduces its powers to punish those attempting suicide. This was a landmark move, as the act recognises that suicide is triggered by psychological stressors and not criminal intentionality. It also ensures access to care, treatment and rehabilitation for those in psychological distress. The decriminalisation of suicide has also paved the way for a more sensitive and humane approach to the complexities of suicide and resulted in more extensive reporting and better epidemiology. These changes have translated into greater resource allocation for informed public health policy and practices to address this serious but preventable public health issue. However, we are yet to implement a comprehensive National Suicide Prevention strategy, despite ongoing efforts to make this a reality.

In the past century, there has been remarkable progress in the field of mental health, which has expanded our knowledge of suicide as well. It is well known that mental health conditions such as depression are a risk factor in suicide. Unlike in the West, where 90 per cent of suicides are associated with mental health issues like depression, only 60 per cent of people who die by suicide in India have an associated mental health issue. Yet, it is a matter of serious concern. According to data from the National Crime Records Bureau, from 1999 to 2010, the percentage of suicides due to mental illness increased from 4.8 to 7 per cent.

In 2012, the WHO designated India as the suicide epicentre of Southeast Asia. Young people in India face many trials growing up, including the stress of having to live up to exacting parental and societal expectations. Additionally, they live in a society where, despite evidence that indicates it needs to be studied further, suicide is still not completely understood. We see suicide victims being branded as weak, selfish and cowardly. Or, at the other extreme, they are glorified and romanticised as 'heroes'. We think that they choose to 'take the way out' of a problem. We also tend to believe that only 'certain types of people' or people in marginalised communities, who face so many difficulties in everyday life, die by suicide. We try to find tangible reasons for suicide that make sense to us. But the issues connected to suicide are complex and in need of careful attention. Anyone can be affected by a mental health issue irrespective of their economic conditions, financial security, family situation and status in society. Anyone can die by suicide.

Given its powerful impact on society, WHO now recognises suicide as a public health priority and has made raising awareness about suicide and suicide prevention a high priority in the global public health agenda.

Survivors of suicide loss are often invisible and marginalised. Because of the stigma around suicide, they encounter blame, judgement or social exclusion. Annually, across the world, it is said that almost 14.4 million people deal with suicide bereavement: for every suicide, there are approximately 18 people who experience a difficult life disruption. One would not expect something so common or widespread to be shrouded in public stigma.

Survivors of suicide loss face two types of stigma. Public stigma refers to 'the phenomenon of large social groups endorsing negative stereotypes about and acting against a stigmatised group'. It is often coupled with self-stigma, whereby individuals think they are being devalued (that is, perceived stigma) and thus experience all the elements of stigma. Nor is this a recent phenomenon. It can be traced back to a time when people who died by suicide were often denied proper burial and their family's property was snatched away.

On 27 April 2018, Murali's first death anniversary, I launched SPEAK at a quiet function in American College, Madurai. My parents were present, and so were my close friends and well-wishers, who had journeyed with me through the tumultuous year. An initiative to prevent suicide and promote mental health, SPEAK is part of the MS Chellamuthu Trust and Research Foundation—the largest mental health services provider in south Tamil Nadu, focused on making mental health care available, accessible and affordable to all, especially for people in low-income groups.

SPEAK was composted in my grief, pain and anguish. It was watered with my tears of sorrow and pain. It emerged organically, guided by my journey and the vision of a suicide-free world where mental health and well-being would be a way of life. We are driven by our mission to prevent needless deaths due to suicide, and to do that, we create safe supportive spaces for informed conversations on suicide and mental health.

My inspiration to start SPEAK was Shanthi Ranganathan, the iconic psychiatric social worker who set up the TT Ranganathan Clinical Research Foundation, Chennai, after she lost her husband to alcohol dependence. In the late 1970s, alcohol dependence was mired in stigma, as it continues to be even now. Dr Ranganathan addressed this by studying how to treat and rehabilitate persons with substance dependence, and shortly thereafter set up the TT Ranganathan Clinical Research Foundation in the garage of her home. Since then, it has evolved into a centre, in collaboration with WHO, for the treatment and rehabilitation of people with dependence on alcohol and other addictive substances. Lived experience often has the potential to catalyse personal growth and transformation, and for Dr Ranganathan, it was also a tool for social change.

I had the opportunity to interact with Dr Ranganathan when I wrote a feature on her for *Housecalls*, a magazine published by the Hyderabad-based Dr Reddy's Laboratories. Her resilience, dignity and personal courage lingered in my memory, and she became my role model after I lost Murali.

Another inspiration has been my former colleague and friend, Priya Babu, who is a transgender activist, theatre artist and author. Priya set up the Transgender Resource Centre in Madurai with meagre resources, backed by an enormous desire to reach out and empower the transgender community.

For the past two years, SPEAK has regularly conducted awareness and sensitisation programmes on suicide prevention for diverse groups of people, from students and teachers to doctors, lawyers and police personnel. Through our workshops, I discovered that the most challenging barrier in suicide prevention is attitudinal. Attitudes, as we know, are the most resistant to change, especially if they have to do with a taboo topic like suicide. We also recently launched SPEAK2us, a mental health line for people in psychological distress, managed by trained volunteers.

'What's the first word you think of when you come across the word suicide?' I ask the audience at every workshop. Without exception, their responses reflect a predominant tendency to view suicide through a moral lens. Connotations of sin and crime are most common, as are cowardice and heroism.

Suicide is not easy to talk about. But I firmly believe that SPEAK needs to engage in radical conversations on the topic to prevent it. One of my friends, a well-known doctor, said to me shortly after Murali's death, 'All of us at some point contemplate suicide. But some of us actually do it.' His words had a ring of comfort to them. It was an honest and upfront admission that, in each of us, the impulse to live and the impulse to die co-exist.

The path to suicide is complex, with several interrelated factors converging. There are fundamental risk factors which could be biological, psychological and environmental. Then there are proximal risk factors that include psychosocial stressors like chronic illness, chronic pain or physical disability, the death of a family member or a close friend, loss of employment or divorce, financial distress, poor academic performance, mental health issues, previous suicide attempts, history of substance abuse, ongoing exposure to bullying, and exposure to discrimination on the basis of gender identity and sexual orientation.

Interestingly, people commonly mistake proximal risk factors as the *cause* of suicide, not understanding that they are oversimplifying a multidimensional issue. Suicide is preceded by suicidal ideation, where individuals feel trapped and hopeless. They experiment with ways to end their pain, and when they find that there is no way to reduce it, they encounter a huge wall of resistance—the typical Hamletian dilemma of 'to be or not to be'. They reach the conclusion that ending their life—which is never pain-free—is a preferable alternative to the pain of living with the psychic ache.

Despite how bleak it appears, there is hope in the field of suicide prevention. Alongside the risk factors are protective factors that decrease the likelihood of suicide ideation and, eventually, suicide. These include connectedness to parents and non-parent adults in the family, academic achievement, access to safe neighbourhoods and schools, supportive peer networks and mentors, awareness of mental health issues and mental hygiene, and overall resilience. The goal of any suicide prevention programme is to mitigate the risk factors and maximise the protective factors; suicides are never impulsive—they progress on a continuum that could be stopped with appropriate intervention.

Keeping this in mind, SPEAK developed a one-day gatekeeper training programme for suicide prevention. A gatekeeper refers to a target individual who has widespread contact with the community. Such people are strategically positioned to recognise a person with suicide risk and to enable at-risk individuals to access appropriate mental health resources. Training helps the gatekeeper acquire the knowledge, attitudes and skills necessary to identify people at risk of suicide, determine levels of risk and make referrals. Although these gatekeepers are mostly non-professionals, they provide a vital link and open the gate between people at risk of suicide and mental health professionals.

SPEAK takes every opportunity to emphasise that suicide is a great leveller that cuts across every possible barrier. Three of my favourite people: Vincent Van Gogh (favourite painter), Ernest Hemingway (favourite author) and Murali (partner and all-around favourite individual), succumbed to suicide. I think it is important that we remember them not for the way they died, but for the lives they led and the legacy they have left behind. That's how I would like to remember Murali and how I would like society to remember him—as a committed professional and a value-driven person. During my conversations with him in 2016, Murali expressed a desire to give back more to society. Perhaps SPEAK will also be a part of his enduring legacy, our joint legacy.

SPEAK Pledge

- I will be a lifelong champion of suicide prevention.
- I will channel my resources to nurture relationships.
- I will create supportive spaces for informed conversations on suicide.
- I will channel my resources to nurture relationships.
- I will reach out to those in distress.
- I will also seek appropriate help while in distress.
- I will do everything possible to ensure everyone's safety.
- I will be better with others instead of better than others.
- I will reach out to people affected by suicide with compassion, concern and empathy.

PART III

A Mother's Search for Meaning

Vasantha Santhanakrishnan is one of my mother's closest friends, and this is her story.

When she lifted the telephone receiver off its cradle on 25 November 1993, her life changed forever. The homemaker and mother of two was staying with her son, who was employed in Indonesia at the time.

'Hello?'

The static on the line overpowered the human voice at the other end. 'Hello? Hello? I am Susheela from Chennai.'

'Hello, Susheela! How are you? *Enna visesham*? Anything special?' Vasantha replied, recognising the voice as that of her friend and neighbour. However, she was puzzled. She had not given her Indonesian number to any of the neighbours. How then had Susheela managed to get it?

Registering Vasantha's bewilderment, her friend said, 'We contacted your son's office in Singapore and got this number.'

The puzzle fell into place. But what had compelled them to do so? An emergency in the family? Health issues to do with her elderly in-laws? Or perhaps it was just a friendly call?

'Hema met with a car accident in Tirupati.'

Vasantha couldn't believe it. Hema? Accident? Not possible.

'Tell me the truth,' she said.

'Hema died by suicide today. We are so sorry.'

A primal scream emerged from the depths of Vasantha's being. She had lost her beloved daughter to suicide.

Just a few months earlier, Hema had been at the Chennai airport, seeing her parents off as they left for Indonesia. Vasantha still remembers the lingering look of sadness on Hema's face—it was her last glimpse of her daughter, when she was alive. Misty-eyed, both mother and daughter had hugged each other. Hema seemed reluctant to disentangle herself from her mother's embrace. After several reluctant-to-let-go moments, she finally said goodbye. Her mother was the only person in the family who had been a sustained source of comfort and strength, especially in the turbulent years preceding and following Hema's marriage.

Hema Surendran, née Santhanakrishnan, was bright, brilliant and bold. She was also beautiful and a dream prospect in the matrimonial bazaar. She had studied mathematics at a well-known college in the city and had also gone on to complete a course in home management and one in computer science as well. She was a yellow belt in karate, played tennis and drove a car.

The Santhanakrishnans were an orthodox Brahmin family from Thanjavur who belonged to the Sri Vaishnavite sect. A close-knit joint family, they had several intergenerational members residing in the same house. When Vasantha was married into the family, it was presumed that she would adapt; she acquiesced and took on the role of a wife, mother and daughter-in-law, excelling in all of them.

Vasantha's husband Santhanakrishnan, an engineer, was then employed with the Indian Railways. After a series of postings in various parts of the country, the couple finally moved to Chennai during the last phase of his tenure. This coincided with the college education of their two children, Hema and her brother.

Hema openly rebelled against the oppressive orthodoxy of the family and was determined to find her wings. 'A cage is a cage, even if it is a golden cage,' she would say. She expressed her desire to enrol for a master's programme in Architecture, but her family opposed the idea of a non-normative career choice for a woman. Having aborted her career plans, the family, in their collective wisdom, decided that it was time for Hema to get married to a boy of their choice.

'I am in love with someone,' said Hema.

The family was scandalised. The prospective groom belonged to another caste from a neighbouring south Indian state. Hema's father was shocked; he thought the differences in education and socio-economic status between the two young people was an unbridgeable chasm. Nevertheless, Hema was determined to marry Surendran, the man she was in love with.

Santhanakrishnan reasoned with his daughter. He begged, cajoled and pleaded. He even offered to send her abroad for higher studies if it would help her 'get over' what he clearly perceived to be an 'infatuation'.

Hema, however, refused to budge. The family reluctantly gave in. However, Santhanakrishnan and his family, including the extended family, never forgave Hema for her transgression.

Love, they say, is a salve for the soul. Their wedding card, which Hema's mother still preserves, read:

> Once in a lifetime, someone special meets someone special.
> Life begins to find a special meaning, dreamy and distant.
> Dazzling damsel, special friend ... A celebration!

The euphoria was poignantly short-lived. Within a couple of months, Hema was back at her parents' place.

'I admit I made a mistake,' she said. The marriage was a disaster. The incompatibility was insurmountable. With the sort of wisdom that only comes in retrospect, Hema decided she wanted to opt out of a toxic marriage. The family blamed her for the impulsive decision to marry the boy despite their well-intentioned warnings.

'While I do agree that the rest of the family had a good reason to feel the way they did, there is no point holding on to the past. Yes, my daughter could have listened to us. But what happened had happened. We could have been supportive and helped Hema rebuild her life,' Vasantha says ruefully, twenty years after Hema's suicide.

The loss of a child is a crushing burden for any parent. However, losing a child to suicide amplifies the sorrow. It is perceived as doubly transgressive: conventional wisdom holds that children are to outlive their parents; however, in a suicide, children not only jump the queue, they also decide when to call it quits. Societal norms mandate that parents are responsible for their children. A child's suicide is often perceived as a moral flaw, and the inability of parents to have prevented the death is highlighted. Among the host of reasons that are attributed is the abdication of parental responsibility. This prevailing negative stereotype is often internalised by parental survivors of suicide as self-blame or an exaggerated sense of responsibility for not having saved their child.

In the immediate aftermath of the tragedy, Vasantha, like most survivors of suicide loss, was swamped with anger—directed towards herself, her daughter and the rest of her family. She experienced guilt, self-blame and an overpowering sense of shame.

'I felt I had failed in my duty as a parent and was angry with myself for being so non-assertive and not speaking up for my daughter,' recalls Vasantha, while conceding that she was unable to challenge the collective orthodoxy and rigidity of her family. At the same time, she was angry with her daughter for having abandoned the family and betrayed them.

'Why didn't she think of us? How could she do this to us?'

The truth is that, among women in India, marital conflicts are a significant risk factor, and the country has the highest percentage of suicides—37 per cent—among women.

'As parents, we failed to inspire confidence in our daughter. We needed to have empowered her, enabled her to face life's challenges. Since we did not do any of this, ending her life was the only option ...' Vasantha tells me. She pauses, her eyes misting up with the endless self-flagellation. 'That was her destiny ... Destiny cannot be changed,' she adds, philosophising her pain and loss.

Perhaps these moments of self-reflection grant the distraught parent a brief reprieve from the vicious cycle of self-blame and reproach.

For nearly two years, Vasantha and her husband lived in self-imposed isolation. The couple were mutually supportive through the tragedy and emerged as each other's strongest source of solace. 'I requested my sister-in-law to take care of my mother-in-law, and my husband and I lived apart from the rest of the family,' Vasantha says.

Although Vasantha denies being compelled to cover up or invent a socially acceptable reason for her daughter's death, she nevertheless experienced the stigma of being branded as a mother whose daughter had ended her life. The whispers, the sidelong glances and the occasional frontal assault invaded her privacy constantly and were a regular occurrence at social gatherings, especially weddings.

'I was often the object of pity, curiosity and gossip.'

Not surprisingly, the couple dealt with the social isolation and empathy deficit by withdrawing into a cocoon.

Despite being a devoutly religious person, for two years after the tragedy, Vasantha lost all faith in religion. She began to avoid temples. Hadn't her gods failed to prevent the catastrophe despite her unswerving devotion and faith? However, this turned out to be a coping strategy to deal with the paralysing shock of the tragedy. As soon as the numbness wore off and the challenges of renegotiating life made their presence felt, re-engaging with religion became a salve for her beleaguered self.

'My husband and I began to regularly attend lectures on Vedanta conducted by the Sri Ramakrishna Math and the Chinmaya Mission. Reconnecting with the divine filled us with so much peace. It was like finding a safe harbour after a turbulent voyage,' recalls Vasantha.

In addition, the couple discovered other ways to sublimate their pain. They became involved with orphanages and organisations for children with special needs, often volunteering their time and supporting the centres financially. Vasantha also volunteered for the crisis helpline of Sneha, a well-known suicide prevention NGO based in Chennai.

Vasantha understands that there is no timeline for grief after such a devastating loss. Undoubtedly, all these years later, the grief is no longer as raw and visceral. The ocean is no longer turbulent, but eddies and whirlpools still lurk beneath the deceptively placid waters.

Vasantha says, 'I will forever grieve for Hema, nothing can take that pain away. It will stay with me for as long as I live.' She realises that while it is important to move through the loss, it is impossible to move on. Hema will forever be the missing person in the family photograph, a phantom limb whose absence will always be felt by the grieving mother.

Today, Vasantha's son is married, and she is a doting grandparent to two lovely young grandchildren. Yet, there is a lingering sense of sadness. She says that there is a deep void inside her, which neither time nor distance has softened or blurred.

'That *yaekkam*, the lingering sense of longing and loss that is part of my life, I've learnt to live with it. We need to move forward and through the loss, but this does not mean that we forget them. We carry them inside us for ever. We need a lot of *mana dhairyam*—mental courage—and faith in a higher power. We need to live our *swadharma* and discover our purpose in life, for which we are on this planet,' says Vasantha, embodying Vedantic wisdom.

Like most survivors of suicide loss, Vasantha's life can be divided into two phases: before and after the suicide. After the initial overwhelming period of grief and despair, she is now rooted in a 'new normal'. She has learnt to live and laugh and participate in life. She has also discovered happiness in the most unlikely places. However, it is a happiness tinged with sorrow. The pain and sorrow have made her infinitely wise and compassionate, though. When she came to condole with me on the death of my husband, her presence was comforting. We developed a strange bond that is unique to those who have lost a loved one to suicide.

'You *will* come through this. You need to now live life on your own terms, don't let others take over your life,' she told me.

Every suicide loss is different, although there are several overlaps. For survivors of suicide loss, support and validation from those with lived experience of a similar loss is deeply reassuring. Vasantha made me see that there are no readymade paths through the wilderness of suicide grief. She also gave me the courage to take the baby steps towards creating my own, often reminding me that 'paths are made by walking'.

No Time to Say Goodbye

Carla discovered her husband's suicide, following which she was 'horrified, filled with disbelief and also angry'.[1] She says, 'I was angry that he had killed himself without saying goodbye or giving me any clues. I felt he had made a huge mistake but I couldn't tell him because he was already dead.'

Like most survivors of suicide loss, until her husband's death, suicide felt 'remote' to Carla. She admits that she had no relationship with it except for news reports about celebrity suicides.

'We were married for 21 years and I thought I knew him. He had obviously been planning his suicide because he bought the anaesthetic he used to inject himself two weeks before his death. So, although I was heartbroken, I also felt betrayed.'

Across the world, every completed suicide is regarded as a crime until proven otherwise. Despite legislation decriminalising suicide, a fatal suicide resembles a crime scene. However, Carla acknowledges that unlike most survivors of suicide loss, she was incredibly lucky. The New York City police and medical examiners were sensitive and kind.

'The police were wonderful with me and it was very clearly a suicide. I went to the local precinct with the detectives and the next day I identified his body after the autopsy. Everyone was very kind and understanding, although they were confused that a

---

[1] Carla's quotes in this chapter are both from her books and her correspondence with me.

physician, a person who saves lives on a daily basis, would take his own life. When I had to identify the body, they gave me orange juice after I fainted. When they returned his items from police headquarters, they expressed their condolences to me. No one seemed to blame me for his suicide, except myself!'

Carla's bereavement was turbulent. She felt bewildered by the primal intensity of the emotions that ambushed her. 'I was not prepared for the violent extremes of emotion that engulfed me after Harry's suicide. In what seemed like seconds, I would careen from feelings of inconsolable sorrow to murderous rage to horrified bewilderment. The reality of what had happened stole my days, relentless nightmares robbed my sleep. I was psychically battered and physically spent.'

The grieving process was challenging in ways that Carla had not anticipated. She became obsessed with an overwhelming desire to solve the mystery of Harry's suicide. She endlessly replayed his death. 'I was going over and over the details of his final minutes, days and hours, not knowing why he did it. If it were an accident, I would have had time to prepare. Also, there is still a great stigma associated with suicide, so Harry's death became more about his suicide than his death.'

Like almost every survivor of suicide loss, Carla too grappled with the dilemma of whether or not to disclose the nature of Harry's death. 'At the beginning, I only told close friends and family. I thought I needed to protect his reputation as a respected physician and initially told his colleagues that he died of a heart attack. But I couldn't and didn't want to keep up the lie. Basically, I'm a terrible liar and kept on telling different stories to different people. It just added to my anxiety.'

Carla also found herself 'championing' her husband. 'I didn't want people to think less of him and I didn't want people to pry into our business,' she says.

A suicide loss, as Carla discovered, irrevocably impacts and alters family dynamics and relationships. Across the world, women survivors of suicide loss are often disproportionately burdened with blame. 'My two older sisters were not supportive; my mother and younger sister were. My brother-in-law blamed me and was very disrespectful to me.' She admits that 'although my sisters cared about me, they really didn't understand what I was going through'.

It also impacted her social networks. 'Harry was a doctor, so I was immediately locked out of any medical meetings, gatherings, etc. My good friends stood by me, but not all did. I had a wonderful friend and co-worker who was by my side the whole time. I dedicated *No Time to Say Goodbye* to him.'

Carla found her lifeline in meeting and interacting with other survivors of suicide loss in New York. She still remembers attending her first support group meeting four weeks after Harry's death, on his birthday. Even that was initially challenging.

'Since Harry's suicide, I felt increasingly isolated from my friends and family. They had no idea what I was going through, all their well-intentioned advice and words of comfort seemed ignorant at best and tinged with cruelty at worst. Here I was with others who had supposedly experienced the nightmare of suicide and I still felt alone and disconnected. Trapped and claustrophobic, I started to leave without even removing my coat.'

It was the facilitator of the support group who persuaded Carla to stay. 'You are among friends,' he reassured her. Listening to group members share how the loss of their loved one to suicide impacted them and how they rebuilt their lives was transformative for Carla. It enabled her to normalise suicide grief and realise that it could happen to anyone. She came to understand that people who died by suicide were not sinners or criminals, but were just people in great pain.

'Only other survivors of suicide loss knew what I was feeling. Had all the people in this room, these normal people, really been through suicide? Did they all feel as guilty as I did? Were their lives, too, shredded beyond recognition? Ever since Harry died, I have found great comfort in these groups.'

A support group for survivors of suicide loss offers a safe space for people to reclaim their lives and move towards healing. Like Carla discovered, the simple act of listening to others share their experience is an antidote to the stigma, shame, secrecy and silence experienced by survivors of suicide loss.

Carla also sought individual therapy to process her traumatic grief. She says that she was lucky to have a therapist who was 'enthusiastic about the groups; she was not threatened by the self-help nature of their structure but viewed them as an essential ingredient in my healing process.'

Carla does not mince words. She says that it is 'imperative' for survivors of suicide to get help to rebuild their lives. This could be support groups, individual therapy, family counselling or spiritual comfort. 'Unfortunately, the interest of the mental health profession centres on people who commit suicide, not on those of us who are left behind to deal with its consequences.'

The moral aversion and horror when it comes to suicide has other far-reaching effects on the surviving family members. Clara writes eloquently about the disenfranchised grief of those bereaved by suicide. They cannot openly talk or acknowledge it; they are subject to relentless speculation and interrogation about why and how it happened.

'In my mourning, I too wanted to be like everyone else. I wanted my family and friends to comfort me, not to question me about why Harry had killed himself. I wanted to grieve my husband's absence, not analyse his reasons for dying. I wanted to celebrate his kindness and friendship during our 21 years of marriage, not to rage at him for abandoning me in the prime of our lives.'

Carla began to rebuild her life by starting to write again. 'I began to read as much as I could about how suicide affects those who have been left behind and why people kill themselves. I didn't want Harry's death to be in vain. I knew that if I wrote a book about it and talked to survivors across the world about their pain, it would help me as well.'

'Before the loss—I was 43 years old then—I didn't think that the world could change in a nanosecond; after the suicide, I know that nothing is certain,' Carla says. 'While journeying through the wilderness of suicide grief, I lost my innocence, but I gained knowledge. And no matter how much you may love someone, you can't will their life spirit over to them. Suicide is very humbling.'

Over the years, Carla's wound has healed, although the scars persist, perhaps will forever. 'The support of loving people, including my future husband, whom I married seven years after Harry's death, helped me rebuild my life. I have incorporated Harry's life into mine as much as I could.'

Carla is clear that her husband's death by suicide has changed her life irrevocably. She will never be the same person again. There is no going back, only a going forward and accepting that the past can be honoured, but can never be recreated.

'Unlike our loved ones, whose pain was so enveloping that they were unable to hear our shouts of help, we refuse to be exiled by despair. As we reach out to others, we discover inner strengths we never knew existed. Although we did not ask for this test of our endurance—and would reverse the circumstances if given the choice—we discover that we are more resilient, less afraid, more empathetic and understanding as a result of what has happened to us. In a journey filled with unfamiliar landmarks and unexpected turns, those of us whose loved ones have ended their lives so abruptly and with such anguish do not waver from one unassailable certainty. We dearly miss our mothers and sisters, our husbands and daughters, our brothers and sons, our wives and fathers, our relatives and friends. Yes, our survival and even our triumph is the legacy we now carry forward, a testament to the memory of those we have loved and inexplicably lost.'

Carla has been the lighthouse in my own journey through oceanic grief. Her wisdom, compassion and sisterhood have empowered me to live a life of authenticity.

The Neglected Mourner

My friend Sudha has an M.Phil. in English Language and Literature, and was a successful teacher for many years. Following marriage and motherhood, she chose to be a homemaker. However, after her children had flown the nest, life threw a curveball at her. Her apparently stable marriage broke down.

Never one to be cowed by life's challenges, Sudha reinvented herself professionally by taking on a demanding and hugely challenging examination and clearing it successfully at the age of fifty-one. All through this period, I remember being struck by her avowed disinterest in, and refusal to read, any books in the philosophy and self-help genres.

Today, as I connect the dots, I am no longer flummoxed by Sudha's divergent choices.

It was May, and the weather in Kerala was pre-monsoonish. A muggy stillness cloaked the air. Black-grey storm clouds hovered menacingly on the horizon, threatening to deluge the landscape. The backwaters of Kollam, the picturesque coastal city in Kerala, were deceptively calm.

Sudha gazed languidly at the furrowed surface of the backwaters, soaking in the tranquillity. As the train rumbled to a halt at the junction, she clambered out of the compartment. Squinting her eyes, she scanned the platform to see if her father had come to take her home. Instead, she saw familiar silhouettes that she recognised as her uncle and her cousin. She quelled the gnawing uneasiness at her dad's absence. Perhaps he had unavoidable work engagements, she reasoned.

'My parents' home was chaotic when we reached. There was a huge crowd outside. People were wailing and howling. I wondered if something had happened to either of my parents. Then someone told me that my brother Anand had killed himself …'

Like every survivor of suicide loss, Sudha's life was instantly divided into the time before and after Anand's suicide. As his elder sister, she had watched Anand grow into a brilliant student. He joined a Sainik School on a full scholarship in class six. However, two years later, while in class eight, he refused to go back to school after the summer holidays. Why her brother was adamant about not going back remained a mystery, but Sudha suspects now that he may have been bullied or harassed.

Both siblings were academically bright. But Sudha always felt that her parents favoured her brother. 'He was the apple of their eye,' she says, the hurt still evident in her voice.

Anand's behaviour at home was unpredictable. His violent outbursts and wild mood swings became difficult for Sudha to cope with as time passed. 'I remember how he once pulled away the towel I had wrapped around my head and tightened it around my neck. I was unable to breathe. I was horrified and decided not to stay at home after that day,' she recalls. Home felt increasingly unsafe.

Life offered her a reprieve when she moved to another city for her post-graduation. Anand also enrolled for an undergraduate degree in English in another state. For a while, it seemed that the siblings bonded over their field of study. 'We vibed well with each other, and there were many shared moments we treasured as siblings,' says Sudha. 'Anand wrote the most beautiful poems with

Keatsian overtones. I still have them with me and treasure them. We chatted often during my previous visit in January.'

Yet, his intense, brooding nature and existential angst overwhelmed Sudha. She felt that she lacked the vocabulary to make sense of Anand and his psychological landscape. In retrospect, she admits that he might have been dealing with a psychological issue like depression, but back then, neither she nor her parents thought of this as a possible reason for his inexplicably bizarre behaviour.

'Nobody could talk to Anand,' Sudha says. 'He inhabited a place to which no one in the family had access. I still remember the date I saw him for the last time, 21 January 1990. I had not thought much about suicide. Until then, I had not heard of anyone who had lost their life to suicide.'

A suicide is never a self-contained act, Sudha discovered. Suicide loss skews the sense of perspective. It erodes the sense of discrimination and discernment, and steers one to make decisions that one regrets later.

The loss of a sibling is profound. It ruptures the fabric of a shared childhood. 'Siblings shape your ancestry and sense of self. They are often the forgotten mourners in suicide loss,' writes Julie Cerel, psychologist and president of the American Suicidology Association.

A sibling is supposed to be an absolute constant in one's life. Death by suicide shatters this notion. It also changes the family dynamics and irrevocably alters the equation between the parents and the surviving child.

'I was studying in another city. Whenever I went home, I would find my mother in tears, even months after it had happened. Their intense grief got to me, and I worried about them,' says Sudha.

While it was true that her parents were grappling with an extraordinarily traumatic loss, Sudha's grief was equally intense. Yet, she experienced little validation of her grief within the family.

'My parents coped very poorly. My mom was constantly crying, she was inconsolable. When Anand was there, he was the apple of their eye; now that he was gone, I felt I didn't matter to them as much as he did. In a way, I felt isolated and neglected.'

To assuage her grief, Sudha found support and love in her teachers at college and her wide circle of friends.

'My being away from my parents and having my own set of friends helped a lot. Looking back, I feel that I tried too hard to have fun with my friends. I also spoke about him a lot; speaking gave me solace. In a way, I was proud of that little soul who had decided that he could no longer live in this world that is unfair in all aspects.'

When Sudha was able to openly talk about her pain and the anguish of her bereavement, her friends listened attentively. She felt validated and visible as a mourner, realising that she too had the right to grieve. This was possible because she was surrounded by a circle of unconditional love and support.

However, the process of grieving was not easy. 'The attitude of the people around me made it particularly challenging,' Sudha says. 'I remember that I had gone out with my best friend a month after my brother died, and someone gossiped about it, saying that it was inappropriate for me to be laughing after having lost my brother. I was shocked when I came to know about this.'

Within six months of Anand's death, her parents made a rather unusual decision—to adopt a baby boy. They were in their forties then.

'I wouldn't say my attitude towards life changed in any way due to this loss. But my whole life was upended due to certain decisions that my parents took subsequently. I feel that my parents' intense sense of loss made them adopt a baby boy and shower him with a lot of love, while not caring much about my future. This overcompensating behaviour affected me a lot,' Sudha admits.

Sudha was twenty-two years old then and in love with a man whom she was going to marry. Her fiancé and his family opposed the adoption. 'In desperation, I wrote a letter to my parents begging them to delay the adoption at least until the marriage had taken place. After all, I agreed with friends and family who said that as I was to get married shortly, they could find joy in the grandchildren. Sadly, the letter reached them after they brought the baby home. When Anand was there, he was everything to them. Now, it was Naren. I was never in their field of vision,' she sighs.

The engagement was called off. Sudha sought solace in one of her friends, Mohan, who had always been supportive of her. It began as a casual friendship that soon blossomed into a campus romance and, eventually, marriage.

'I was able to bounce back and move forward once I became closer to Mohan, the person I later got married to. He was a huge support,' says Sudha.

After two decades of a stable and fulfilling marriage, Sudha and Mohan got divorced.

Over the years, Sudha has managed to move through the traumatic pain and loss. She is a remarkably resilient woman and a committed parent. But she still wonders whether her brother's suicide is the reason the rest of her life was filled with so many challenges. Or, she wonders, is abandonment the leitmotif of her life?

Sudha sees startling similarities between Anand and her son, Prem. Like Anand, Prem is a brilliant student of English Literature. Like his uncle, he is given to intense brooding and philosophising about life and living.

'There are times when my son talks of suicide. While I understand where it comes from, I sometimes deplore such talk. He knows that I am always there for him,' says Sudha.

Sudha still does not read any self-help or philosophy as she feels that the time Anand spent reading these had only intensified his brooding and sense of alienation.

The Psychiatrist as a Survivor of Suicide Loss

'It took me ten years to cry after I lost my father to suicide,' Dr Mohan Raj, a well-known psychiatrist, tells me.

I first met him in 2017, when I attended a group-process workshop where he was a co-facilitator. 'Coming out' of the closet of suicide grief, I chose to bare my naked vulnerability in the safe, supportive space created by the group. The intense one-hour processing was incredibly cathartic and liberating. At the end of it, Dr Mohan Raj shared with all of us that he too was a survivor of suicide loss.

His honesty and courage in owning his vulnerability helped me realise that suicide bereavement can happen to anyone. Even psychiatrists. Until then, I had only heard of psychiatrists who had lost patients to suicide, but here was one who had lost his father to it. The 'wounded healer' had healed and transformed after the tragedy.

Thursday, 3 November 1994. The day Dr Mohan Raj heard of his father's suicide. He was working as a faculty senior resident after completing a residency in Psychiatry at the country's premier mental health institute.

'When I heard my father had died, I knew it was a suicide,' he recalls. His father had struggled with a serious case of depression for a long time.

Less than a month prior, Dr Mohan Raj had visited his parents in southern Tamil Nadu. He and his wife were expecting a baby, and he wanted to pick up some handmade towels, for which the town was renowned.

'I was concerned to see my father seriously depressed. He was confined to his room, seemed aloof and withdrawn and had even attempted to end his life recently. I started him on anti-depressant medication and wanted to take him back with me for intensive treatment after the birth of our child,' Dr Mohan Raj says. 'I thought he would come around in two weeks.'

Ironically, the anti-depressant made his father 'well enough to act but not for the suicidal ideas to disappear'.

Like every survivor of suicide loss, Dr Mohan Raj felt 'numbed, shocked and incredibly sad' upon hearing the tragic news. 'I also felt a strange sense of relief that my father's agony was over. The anger and the guilt came much later,' he says. Unlike many survivors of suicide loss, he was not filled with disbelief when he heard the news.

The fourteen-hour bus journey home for the funeral was a time for retrospection, occasionally tinged with self-reproach and self-blame. Should he have been more responsible for his father's well-being? Shouldn't he have noticed the red flags and acted appropriately to save his life? Wasn't that part of his training as a psychiatrist?

He was assaulted by conflicting emotions. 'I remember my father as a highly anxious and indecisive person. As a psychiatrist, I assessed my father for suicidal risk, since he was severely depressed. However, I never thought he could kill himself. Yet, I felt proud that my father "could" make such an important decision, to end his life. He was not as timid as we believed him to be, after all.'

By the time he reached home, his father had been cremated because the body had begun to decompose. 'I handled the aftermath of the tragedy clinically. There was no emotion. The police, the post-mortem report, the investigations ... I was completely in charge and interfaced with the police. And no, I didn't cry. I'm surprised I didn't cry at all.'

Throughout the ordeal, a senior professor's advice kept him anchored. 'He said to me, "Watch your moods. Take adequate care of yourself. And most important, don't feel guilty for not having prevented the death."'

In the middle of all this, Dr Mohan Raj's wife gave birth to a baby girl.

'I felt as though my father could have lived to see the child. Why was there such a hurry for him to go? I was angry with him. It was a very auspicious time, we were expecting our first baby … He could have stayed and shared our joy. Wasn't it selfish of him to end his life just then?'

'At that time, I was a logical, cerebral person. There was no place for emotions in my life. So, I looked at the whole thing through a clinical gaze,' admits Dr Mohan Raj.

When he returned to work, a colleague had invented a socially acceptable reason for the death. He told people that Dr Mohan Raj's father had succumbed to a sudden heart attack.

'I felt uncomfortable when I heard this. After all, everyone in my immediate circle knew the reason. Why was there a need to hide it? Truth is truth and needs to be told. Had he checked with me, I would have encouraged him to tell the truth. However, by then, my daughter was born. While colleagues condoled with me, most of the discussion was about the baby!' It was easy for him to avoid being trapped in a situation, he says, where people would probe the reason for the death or ask other intrusive, investigative questions that most survivors of suicide loss have to confront.

His father's death was public because of how he had killed himself. The family, therefore, had no choice but to acknowledge the death as suicide. Dr Mohan Raj still wonders: had his father's method of death been less explicit, would they have covered up the cause of death and passed it off as due to natural causes?

The suicide of a loved one had repercussions on Dr Mohan Raj's professional life too. He says that the lived experience of suicide loss has made him more sensitive and compassionate to both suicide survivors and survivors of suicide loss.

'I took extra care of patients who were depressed and ensured that they were closely monitored for suicidal risk,' he explains. His hypervigilance, he says, was always countered by his harsh inner critic who constantly mocked and taunted him. 'What sort of a psychiatrist are you? You could not save your father and now you are trying to save others?'

For years, Dr Mohan Raj felt tormented for not having saved his father. He also became more cautious and attentive when treating patients with depression who were around his father's age when he died. A crushing sense of guilt weighed him down. 'It was a blot on my character. Here I was … a psychiatrist to the rest of the world, unable to save my own father!' he says, the sense of irony and anguish palpable in his voice.

His perceived filial failure also impacted his self-image of professional competence. 'I resolved the guilt of not having prevented the death. Before that, because I had failed to prevent the death, I felt that I was not a good son, a good psychiatrist, and therefore I did not deserve the good things in life. I constantly denied myself pleasure because I felt I just didn't deserve it. Psychotherapy helped me connect these two important dots and set myself free. I learnt that, no matter how much we do for others, ultimately, each one of us is only responsible for our own life. That was a turning point for me and it brought such tremendous relief!'

Today, when he assesses a patient with depression for suicidal risk, Dr Mohan Raj says he is able to do so as a psychiatrist who blends clinical acumen with compassion and concern. 'It doesn't spring from guilt or a feeling of having failed in my duty as a son. I no longer connect it to Appa at all. It's not as if I've let him go, so let me do a *prayaschitham*, atonement, for my perceived sense of not having been responsible enough.

'Earlier, I thought that using my cognition and not being emotional—like a rock—was my strength. Later, I realised that being in touch with my vulnerabilities and emotions is my strength.'

Playing Hide and Seek with Sorrow

Dhananjayan, our driver, has been with us for more than two decades. We call him DJ, and he is very much a part of our family. When DJ spoke of his relationship with his boss and how his tragic death had impacted him, I realised his maturity and wisdom. He remembers Murali for the person he was, not for the manner of his death. Listening to him, it occurred to me that people like DJ have the power to foster compassionate conversations on suicide.

On 28 April 2017, when DJ met me at the Madurai station and drove me home, there was nothing to suggest that my life was about to change forever. As always, I asked him about Murali. He told me that he had met my husband the previous evening and that he had been preparing for a talk at a state-level urology conference. Murali had met a senior lawyer in the city to get his inputs. He had asked DJ to request Ishwari, the domestic worker in our house, to cut some fruit.

'He talked as usual with me. I did not sense anything unusual in his mood or behaviour. On the morning of 28 April, I came to the house to pick up the car and drive to the station. Malli and Minnal were outside. I did not find it unusual because sometimes Dr Murali would let them out if they wanted to go outside. I thought he must have been sleeping inside the house,' recalls DJ.

When I had shrieked on discovering Murali's body, DJ had gingerly entered the room. In retrospect, his movements strike me as robotic. It was as if time had stood still.

'I walked into the bathroom. Our beloved doctor was lying on his side in the bathroom. One look and I knew it was all over,' recalls DJ with tears in his eyes. 'I closed the bathroom door as I knew the police would investigate. And also the bedroom door. I cried like a little child who had lost his parent. I felt orphaned and alone. One part of me felt numb. At the same time, I was crying uncontrollably. I wondered if my tears would ever stop flowing.'

It would be an understatement to say that DJ was in a state of shock. 'I could not accept the fact that Dr Murali had ended his life. I believe that after his wife, I was the one who understood him the most. I had been supportive in every way I could. There was no urologist who could match his knowledge and skills. He had everything a person could want in life: name, fame, a loving wife. What didn't he have? Why did he have to do this? When my younger son, Nilavan, was ill with meningitis, Dr Murali had taken care of all his medical expenses. When Nilavan died, Dr Murali was my support and strength and helped me come to terms with the loss. However, now, I found myself crying for him even more than I cried for Nilavan. Who will comfort me now?'

His employer's death was DJ's first encounter with suicide. 'It was the first time I had seen a death by suicide. Losing a loved one to suicide is most painful. Until then, I had only read or heard of suicide in the media. It was just a news item in the newspaper or on TV.'

Three years later, DJ still talks of Dr Murali in the present tense. Memories of him and the conversations he had with him still linger, as though they happened recently.

Murali was full of concern for his welfare, says DJ. 'Dr Murali always sat in the front seat when I drove. He once said to me, "For a doctor and a driver, hands and legs are the most important. So, take proper care of yourself and drive carefully. If you die, the loss is irreplaceable for your family." I said to him, "Sir, if I die, only my family will suffer. But if you die, it is a loss for society itself."

He patted me on the shoulder and said with a big smile, "Oh, like that, is it? *Sari,* da! Then let's both be happy and live long!"

On the day of Murali's death, DJ says he recalled this advice and every other piece of advice Murali had given him. 'He was full of practical wisdom, I listened to every word he had to say. How could he do this to himself?'

Murali was a public figure, well-known in Madurai and in the rest of India. Hence, DJ says, he made a bold decision to tell the truth about his death. However, he made a nuanced distinction between privacy and secrecy. Knowing DJ as I do, I am hardly surprised at his pragmatic wisdom, uncluttered by bookish knowledge.

'When people asked me about the death, I admitted it was suicide. But I did not divulge details such as the manner of death. I felt that hiding the real cause of the death would not be good for him. After all, there was nothing in his life to be ashamed of. On the other hand, he touched so many lives as a doctor.'

DJ, like me, is a survivor of suicide loss. The impact of Murali's death on him helped me realise that survivors of suicide loss do not necessarily have to have a kinship with the deceased. The relationships can also be non-kinship, like those of an employee, a friend or a healthcare professional. The defining factor is the intimacy and emotional connect in the relationship.

Apart from being a suicide loss survivor like me, DJ was also a victim of insensitive and intrusive enquiry by the law enforcement authorities, which bordered on harassment and intimidation. 'All that actually added to my stress and made it worse. Even for a lay person like me, it is obvious that there is a lot of difference between a death by suicide and a non-suicidal death,' he says.

Murali's death affected DJ in multiple ways—physical, emotional and psychological. His grief in the acute phase was eerily similar to mine. 'For about three months, I could not sleep or eat properly. I developed stress-related diabetes, a stomach ulcer, and my blood pressure was higher than usual. Memories of

Dr Murali flooded my mind. I felt he was alive. I felt empty and cried inconsolably.'

Fortunately, DJ is surrounded by supportive people. 'My wife and son were most supportive. They insisted that I must continue working here. I agreed with them because from the day Dr Murali died, I began to see him through your eyes,' he tells me. 'Your brother Venkatesh and your parents were also supportive. You often counselled me and helped me cope with my grief. Your positive outlook and strength inspired me. Sometimes, when I wanted to talk about Dr Murali but didn't want to burden you, I would ring up your brother, who was another source of support and strength.'

DJ wistfully admits that Murali's death reconfigured his life, both internally and externally. 'I am no longer the same person. I realise that nothing is certain in life. My social circle has reduced. I don't feel like meeting too many people. I prefer to interact with just a few close friends, because for most people in our society, a suicide death is a source of gossip and I want to avoid that. I have become more compassionate, caring and sensitive to other people's pain. In my own way, I try to do the best I can for such people—give them hope and strength, and enable them to acquire *mana pakkuvam*, equanimity of mind.'

When I listened to DJ's account of healing through grief, I was impressed by his profound insights into the grieving process and his robust resilience.

'The sorrow of Dr Murali's death will stay with me as long as I live. The sorrow continues to play hide and seek with me. It would be foolish to think that one day it will go away. However, day by day, I am learning to accept this harsh truth. Dr Murali was unmatched both personally and professionally. His character and ethics were unparalleled. His patient care, concern and commitment were inspirational. He would go to work even if he was unwell. I learnt so many things from him—how to be organised, how to save, how to spend wisely ... He opened my first bank account in 1999 and told me that it was important to develop the habit of regular savings.'

DJ's relationship with Murali was based on mutual respect, love and affection. In his last letter to me, written just before his death, Murali had instructed me to give DJ a generous amount of money. I felt overwhelmed by his foresight and thoughtfulness. DJ truly deserved this heartfelt 'thank you' from his long-time employer and mentor.

'I was truly touched by his generosity. I was even more touched when his last wish was carried out as soon as the fifteen-day mourning ended. Dr Murali is *deivam* (god) to me. Even god comes next only to him,' says DJ.

DJ continues to be part of my family. After Murali's death, I told him that he was free to work elsewhere. However, DJ unequivocally chose to stay with me. I am truly grateful for his loving presence in my life. He and I share a deep sibling bond. Needless to say, Murali is a tangible presence in our conversations, and we endlessly rehash memories of the person who remains special to both of us.

Redefining Resilience

My friend Revathi is a trans woman. She is a well-known trans activist, author and performer who lives in Namakkal, Tamil Nadu. Revathi and I collaborated on a book, *A Life in Trans Activism*, which was published in 2016. We interacted closely during the writing of the book. Fearless, frank and feisty, her exemplary resilience inspires me. During one of our interactions, Revathi showed me a picture of a young woman.

'She looks gorgeous! Who is she?' I asked.

'That's Famila. She was my *chela*,' said Revathi with unconcealed pride. 'But in reality, we were like mother and daughter who shared a close relationship and a rare friendship,'

In the hijra community, to which Revathi belongs, it is customary for a young person—known as a *chela*—who has just joined the community to be apprenticed and guided by a senior, the guru. Revathi was Famila's guru. Famila unfolded through Revathi. She was an exceptional communicator, passionate about the rights of the marginalised and vulnerable, a graduate who spoke fluent English and also Revathi's colleague in a well-known rights-based organisation for LGBTQIA+ people. According to Revathi, Famila lived her life based on the principles she believed in. She was the first person from the transgender community who, without fear or hesitation, told the media that she was also a sex worker.

'Until I met Famila, I was ashamed of being a sex worker and felt guilty about it. But Famila helped me realise that by subscribing to such negative stereotypes, I was indulging in self-hatred and self-discrimination—the very aspects of mainstream society that I was trying to address through my advocacy,' recalls Revathi.

Although Revathi was older and senior to her, and was the person Famila turned to for advice and support, Revathi recalls that it also worked the other way. 'Famila was a source of solace and strength to me. When I was going through a personal crisis and felt suicidal, she provided me the support and gently encouraged me to rebuild my shattered life and look forward to a future with optimism and hope. There was nothing I did not share with her. She knew my highs and lows, my dreams and desires, my shadows and fears.'

'Mummy! Tell me the recipe for radish chutney.' It was Famila on the phone.

'I gave her the recipe. It was the last time I heard her voice,' says Revathi with a sigh. The subsequent years did not dim her pain. They only made it bearable.

'Around midnight on 17 July 2004, I got a call from Famila's partner. Famila had killed herself. My world stopped. I was numb. I did not know how to react. I could not believe that the strong, fearless Famila could do this.'

Revathi and her colleagues rushed to the hospital. 'I saw her body in the mortuary. She was wearing a black chemise and tights and looked as if she was sleeping. I touched her body and it still felt warm. I wondered if perhaps there was life still flickering in her. I wondered what I would tell her parents. Suddenly, my heart beat faster and I fainted.'

Famila was just twenty-four when she died. A promising life had been nipped in the bud. Revathi's mind was a cauldron of conflicting emotions—sadness, fear, anger (directed towards herself, Famila, her birth parents, the trans community and society), guilt and self-blame. However, she steeled herself and did what needed to be done. That included making arrangements for the post-mortem and the funeral.

'At Famila's funeral, I performed her last rites. I felt as pained as a birth mother who loses her child. I felt as if I had borne her in my womb for nine months and given birth to her. I wept inconsolably because it should have been her doing this for me. Now, she had jumped the queue and given me this heart-breaking task. Famila's parents and brother had come for the funeral. Her father, who had cut off ties with her, was weeping openly. If only he had accepted Famila, welcomed her back into the family and not cared about society, perhaps his daughter would have been alive today. However, I felt each of us, in some way or the other, individually and collectively, were responsible for Famila's premature and tragic death.'

It has now been sixteen years since Famila's suicide. Yet, Revathi continues with her exploration of why Famila killed herself. 'Famila was such a strong, sensible person. If she had problems, couldn't she have shared them with me? She had so much to give the world. Why did she do this? Wouldn't I have done my best to help and support her?'

Like most survivors of suicide loss, Revathi still performs psychological autopsy as she explores the several possible reasons why Famila killed herself. She is also aware that there were several risk factors for suicide in Famila's life, including earlier self-harm attempts. 'Famila was facing several problems at work and she had quit her full-time job. The generous person that she was, any person who was gender non-conforming was welcome to stay with her until they could afford a place of their own. To support herself and her friends, she began to do full-time sex work. I suppose it took a toll on her, physically and psychologically.'

The pendulum also swings to self-blame and self-recrimination fuelled by the blame foisted on her by other people in her community. 'Many of my community members accused me of having been too liberal and accommodative of Famila's every wish and whim. For instance, Famila loved to wear Western clothes, wake up late, read English books and smoke. Famila was a free spirit. She found it difficult to abide by the strict rules and regulations in our community. Hence, I gave her the freedom and independence to live separately. After her death, my community said that if I had been strict with her, she would be alive today. I wonder if there is some truth in that,' says Revathi, lost in rumination.

Revathi sublimated her intense grief through creative expression. Famila's death was also the beginning of a cascade of unanticipated personal losses in Revathi's life: she lost her job, her marriage broke up, and both her guru and her mother died. She was troubled by frequent intrusive memories of Famila's death. It took nearly two years for her to move through the loss and reshape her life.

'Why do many of my loved ones leave me like this? I began working on my first book in Tamil, *Unarvum Uruvamum* (*The Feelings and the Body*). It was an antidote to the dejection, loneliness and sadness. Meeting so many members of the transgender community and listening to their stories of pain and sorrow made me realise how many things I had to be grateful for. Very soon, my second book in Tamil, *Vellai Mozhi*, which was translated into English as *The Truth about Me*, was also published. After that, I began to travel a lot for book tours and lectures. Meeting so many different people and interacting with them also helped divert the pain.'

Revathi is stoical about the various manifestations of pain in her life, which she says began while she was growing up as a gender non-conforming child. Every instance of trauma, she says, has only made her more resilient.

Today, the searing wound caused by Famila's death no longer haemorrhages as it once did. Revathi has cauterised the bleed with her creativity, activism and philosophical outlook. Yet, there is no telling when the wound will start leaking blood at the seams again. It just takes a little memory to trigger the aching loss.

Suicide loss is usually rendered invisible, glossed over or minimised in the trans community. 'Most suicides in the trans community, unlike those in the non-trans community, are due to intense psychological distress and the stress caused by being perceived as "different" from others,' Revathi says. 'In addition, we face every form of social isolation and exclusion. We are thrown out of our birth homes and schools, bullied, harassed and denied our rights.'

Her observation underscores the conclusion of several studies which highlight that the rate of suicides among trans persons is 40 per cent higher than in other demographic groups.

There is a strange fellowship among those bonded by pain. Four years ago, when Revathi shared the story of Famila's tragic death, I listened with concern and sympathy. I admired her ability to bounce back from life's onslaught. After Murali's death, however, I feel her anguish and sorrow. When I was bereaved, Revathi, who also knew Murali and regarded him highly, consoled me. Her words comforted me. She and I are bonded by our suicide loss. Her resilience continues to inspire me.

Grief Cast in Plaster of Paris

What happens when your psyche is fractured by a tragedy and you apply a cast on it with plaster of paris? As any person with a fractured limb knows, initially the cast is wet, but soon it hardens and exerts a vise-like grip. Some survivors of suicide loss, like Krishnan, who lost his wife to suicide, protect themselves from pain by using a cast for their grief, because that is the only way to prevent themselves from falling apart.

Parenthood seemed elusive for Mahalakshmi and Krishnan. Krishnan says that his wife longed for a baby and remained disappointed and depressed at not being able to conceive. However, fertility treatments finally helped them conceive, and they were overjoyed when they had twin boys ten years after they got married.

But it was a difficult childbirth. Mahalakshmi developed medical complications and was in the intensive care unit (ICU) for a fortnight. The twins too had to be in the ICU for some time. Krishnan's parents stayed with them at the hospital while he was with his wife, who had been shifted to a well-known hospital in a metropolis. To Krishnan's delight, the children and his wife recovered, and life appeared to be good once more. One would have thought that the couple's troubles were over and they would live happily ever after …

Bringing up the twins was challenging for Mahalakshmi. She felt unsupported by her parents. They were busy caring for their younger daughter, who had just had a baby with mental disability. Although Krishnan and his joint family were supportive, Mahalakshmi felt overburdened by two demanding babies.

1 May 2017. Like most survivors of suicide loss, Krishnan remembers that day as if it were just yesterday. He had returned from the vegetable market and was putting away the vegetables in the fridge.

In the village where they lived, it was customary for people to feed infants with donkey's milk, in the belief that it boosted immunity.

'I heard you gave the children donkey's milk. We need to be careful, as we don't know if it is really good for them,' he said casually to his wife.

'So, you know more about bringing up children than I do? Are you implying that I am not a good mother?' she shot back.

'No, ma, I never meant anything like that. It's just that we must be careful, as these are precious babies.'

Silence.

Mahalakshmi went back into the bedroom.

Half an hour later, Krishnan stepped into the room to get ready to leave for work. He found her hanging from the ceiling.

To his shock and horror, Krishnan discovered that his wife was still alive. With the support of the family and neighbours, he rushed her to a nearby hospital. Mahalakshmi struggled for fifteen days before succumbing to the injuries to her heart caused by the trauma.

Today, three years after the incident, the soft-spoken and sensitive Krishnan is still distraught. He wonders how a casual conversation that had no hint of accusation or blame could have triggered his wife's suicide.

'Do people plan to kill themselves or do they do it on an impulse? I was a caring, supportive husband all through the decade of our marriage. Even when we struggled with infertility, I reassured my wife that not having a child was a non-issue. We still had each other.'

In retrospect, he wonders if his wife could have been struggling with a masked depression.

'If she was, I was not aware of it. Perhaps I could have helped her get treated for depression. I would have done anything to prevent this tragedy. She had so much to live for. The children were the centre of her life. How could she do this to herself? How could she abandon the children and me?'

Like every survivor of suicide loss, Krishnan has endless questions but no answers. In the early stages of the bereavement, he was consumed by anger, self-blame and guilt at his inability to have averted the tragedy. Or, as some people would like to believe, for having triggered the tragedy with his innocuous remark.

The police, with their investigative approach, only exacerbated his sense of loss as they relentlessly explored his role in the suicide.

'My parents, brother, my brother's wife and a few close friends were pillars of support in my bereavement. My mother and brother's wife took on the responsibility of caring for the twins. I never thought I would survive the first month. However, my friends reached out unconditionally, and through their love and support, I managed to hold on,' Krishnan says.

Like every survivor of suicide loss, Krishnan learnt to fake it.

'I was unable to cry openly. I hid my tears from my family as they too were overburdened and I did not want to add to that. I had to return to work after a month. I could not share my sorrow with my colleagues as I felt no one really understood what I was going through. Hence, when I would drive to work on my motorbike, I would slip on my helmet and visor and cry my heart out on the highway until the visor turned foggy with tears. When I was overwhelmed at work, I would rush to the bathroom to cry.'

Krishnan says that no one could identify with his pain and anguish—then or now. Over the last three years, he has acquired unbelievable levels of proficiency and expertise in masking his true feelings. The visor he uses has become his *kavach*, armour, that protects him and encases his vulnerability, the fractures and fissures in his psyche, like a permanent plaster of paris cast.

Today, Krishnan is completely involved in parenting his four-year-old twins.

'They are my lifeline and the reason I am holding onto life. If I too end my life, they would be orphaned. I want to give them all my love and affection and ensure that they grow up into responsible, caring adults. Their education is my priority,' he says.

Krishnan sees his role as a single parent as a lifelong commitment to his children. 'I don't want to remarry. I am not sure how the woman I marry will relate to the children,' he says with finality.

Meanwhile, he still cries on his way to work and cries himself to sleep. The pain and anguish are lifelong companions. Will Krishnan be able to leave behind this memory of a monumental tragedy? Or will the memory continue to hold him hostage?

PART IV

The Right to Grieve

> Give sorrow words; the grief that does not speak
> knits up the o'er wrought heart and bids it break.
> —William Shakespeare, *Macbeth*

Fairly early in my grief journey, I stumbled on a pertinent observation by psychiatrist Carl Jung. He said, 'Embrace your grief. For there, your soul will grow.' I found this radical because most of us prefer to avoid confronting grief. Or we simply don't know how to integrate grief into our lives.

Psychotherapist Megan Devine writes about the need to have a deep and meaningful engagement with grief and loss. Eloquently and elegantly, she writes about the accidental death by drowning of her partner in her book *It's OK That You're Not OK: Meeting Grief and Loss in a Culture That Doesn't Understand*.

'Our culture sees grief as a kind of malady: a terrifying messy emotion that needs to be cleaned up and put behind us as soon as possible. As a result, we have outdated beliefs about how long grief should last and what it should look like. We see it as something to overcome, something to fix, rather than something to tend or support. Even our clinicians are trained to see grief as a disorder rather than a natural response to deep loss. When the professionals don't know how to handle grief, the rest of us can hardly be expected to respond with skill and grace.'

Grief psychotherapist, researcher and author Kenneth Doka remarked that grief is about loss, not about death. A bereaved person's world is literally and metaphorically 'ripped apart'. The process of transitioning to a life without the loved one is a journey during which the griever comes to terms with their loss by drawing on their own internal resources, as well as the love and support of their family, friends and community.

Well-known grief psychotherapist Francis Weller, in his lyrical book *The Wild Edge of Sorrow*, says that engaging with grief is 'sacred' work. 'Everyone must take an apprenticeship with sorrow. We must learn the art and craft of grief; discover the profound ways it ripens and deepens us. While grief is an intense emotion, it is also a skill we develop through a prolonged walk with loss.'

In the mid-1980s, Doka coined the term 'disenfranchised grief' to describe the feelings experienced by someone who has been bereaved by non-normative deaths like suicide. There are certain types of grief that can't be openly acknowledged or publicly mourned and are not socially acceptable. In other words, the loss, the grief and the griever are simply not recognised by society. Hence, their grief is not endorsed or validated. Examples of disenfranchised grief include death by suicide, loss or death of a pet, financial loss, infertility, divorce, death of a divorced spouse, a mother giving up a child to adoption, a child's loss of their birth mother, death due to HIV/AIDS and death of a partner who identifies on the LGBTQIA+ spectrum.

Suicide bereavement is complex and complicated. While it resembles the experience of grief after any other kind of death, it is uniquely bewildering and challenging. Survivors of suicide loss are confronted with distinct bereavement issues. The taboo around suicide makes it difficult to talk about the loss, openly acknowledge the cause of death, request social support and publicly mourn the death of the loved one. These aspects of disenfranchised grief make it especially difficult for a survivor to integrate the loss as part of the journey towards healing.

Hence, most survivors struggle to frame a coherent narrative of the loss. They find it difficult to identify people and systems that can validate and normalise the process of grieving. The questions they grapple with may forever remain unanswered. Ironically, acceptance of this ambiguity is a milestone in the healing journey.

Survivors of suicide loss find it difficult to retain any happy memories of the deceased. Unlike with other kinds of death, we feel disconnected from our loved one's legacy and there is a complete absence of joyful nostalgia. Our memories of the deceased person are coloured overwhelmingly by their mode of death.

The convergence of such factors impacts the nature, intensity and duration of suicide grief. Hence, survivors of suicide loss are particularly vulnerable to persistent, complicated, prolonged and traumatic grief. There is a higher risk of suicidal ideation, suicide, major depression, anxiety, post traumatic stress disorder (PTSD), work and social impairment, sleep disturbances, increased risk of cardiac issues and reduced quality of life. This is why counselling and psychotherapy have an important role to play in enabling survivors of suicide loss to transform and heal through their loss. Counselling could be through crisis teams, individual and face-to-face, membership in support groups, and bibliotherapy. I have benefited immensely from support groups—meeting people with similar experiences validated my experience of loss. In addition, once I had healed sufficiently, I was able to return the 'gift of giving'. Support groups, I discovered, are the best 'antidote for the shame of suicide'. As for bibliotherapy, I delved into every book on suicide and suicide loss, including those written by survivors of suicide loss. While the support groups helped me acquire a cognitive understanding of the complex issue of suicide, bibliotherapy, by showcasing lived experiences of survivors of suicide loss, inspired me on my healing journey.

Grief psychotherapy is helpful if you wish to process your grief by seeing it as an organic path to healing and wellness rather than a problem to be fixed. The therapeutic modalities that helped me include gestalt therapy, group process, psychodrama and integral eye movement therapy (IEMT). These modalities are also effective in addressing PTSD. However, there are very few mental health professionals who are trained to support people going through loss and grief. Even fewer are trained to provide support for those who have been bereaved by suicide. Hence, it is quite natural for them to miss, trivialise or deny the uniqueness of suicide grief. In the absence of sensitivity and informed perspectives, they could inadvertently end up endorsing stereotypes about suicide and pathologising suicide grief. The need is for a therapist or counsellor who validates, endorses and supports the unique trajectory of suicide grief. As Doka says, therapists have to 'enfranchise the disenfranchised grief'.

Grieving is both an individual and a collective experience. We need to create spaces that enable people experiencing disenfranchised grief to embrace their grief and to rediscover meaning and purpose in their lives. An empowering and rights-based approach is required to heal their pain and trauma. Such an approach validates their experience and gives them a sense of entitlement to grieve without shame. How does one reclaim the right to grieve? How can one move towards a perspective that normalises suicide grief and recognises the need for it to be seen and heard? Serendipitously, I stumbled upon the Bill of Rights for survivors of suicide loss:

Suicide Loss Survivors' Bill of Rights

- I have the right to be free of guilt.
- I have the right not to feel responsible for the suicide death.
- I have the right to express my feelings and emotions, even if they do not seem acceptable, as long as they do not interfere with the rights of others.
- I have the right to have my questions answered honestly by authorities and family members.
- I have the right not to be deceived because others feel they can spare me further grief.
- I have the right to maintain a sense of hopefulness.
- I have a right to peace and dignity.
- I have the right to positive feelings about the one I lost through suicide, regardless of the events prior to or at the time of the death.
- I have the right to retain my individuality and not be judged because of the suicide death.
- I have the right to seek counselling and a support group to enable me to honestly explore my feelings to further the acceptance process.
- I have the right to reach acceptance.
- I have the right to a new beginning.
- I have the right to be.

What to Say and What Not to Say

> The healing power of the most microscopic exchange with someone who knows in a flash precisely what you are talking about because she experienced that thing too cannot be overstated.
>
> —Cheryl Strayed, *Tiny Beautiful Things: Advice on Love and Life from Dear Sugar*

Most people find it challenging to come up with the right words to condole with a bereaved person. A suicide, however, brings out the worst in people, and those left behind are thus at the receiving end of insensitivity. Cursory condolences are what we get, along with intrusive questions, worn platitudes, hurtful cliches, moralistic branding, all rubbing salt into their cavernous wounds.

I experienced the entire gamut of insensitivity during my bereavement. Of course, it was all 'well intentioned'. Nobody meant to hurt me. Much of it stemmed from lack of empathy and awareness. The inconvenient truth is: nobody knows what to say in such an unusual situation.

When I asserted my right to privacy and expressed my anguish, I was told, 'You are overreacting.' Because there are no guidelines for 'suicide bereavement etiquette', many people stop reaching out for fear of saying the wrong things. How then, instead of minimising, erasing or denying the bereaved person's grief, does one convey concern and compassion? How does one bridge the chasm between intention and expression?

Some norms of suicide bereavement etiquette—based on compassion, concern and care—may help provide a road map to navigate conversations on suicide loss. For instance, don't say, 'I know how you feel.' Or, 'I understand what you are going through.' Suicide grief is a profoundly isolating experience. The truth is that unless you have had a similar experience, you can never really know how a person bereaved by suicide loss feels. Also, no two suicide losses are alike. They may be similar, but not identical. When you say 'I know how you feel' although you have not had a similar experience, you minimise, trivialise or deny the bereaved person's right to grieve. Say, instead, 'I don't know what to say, but I am here for you.' This comes from a space of non-judgement, compassion and concern. And the doors remain open for the kind of honest, authentic communication that is so vital for healing.

Don't ask intrusive questions about the manner and mode of death. During my bereavement, the most frequently asked questions seemed to be, 'How did it happen?' and 'Why did it happen?' Morbid curiosity may be a knee-jerk response to suicide, but it seems to have become normalised.

Don't use hurtful cliches. Phrases such as 'This too will pass', 'You must be strong', 'Everything happens for a reason' and 'You will get over this' trivialise deeply complex circumstances. Avoid doling out such ready philosophies to someone in the throes of suicide bereavement. They don't have the wherewithal to process them and will be overwhelmed. Instead, remember that less is more. Use evocative body language if the person is comfortable with it. You don't need words to make meaning.

Don't assign or imply blame. In your desire to get to the bottom of the story, please do not take on the role of judge and jury. Avoid questions (directly and indirectly) that hold the survivor responsible for the death. Ours is a fishbowl bereavement. Suicide is a public death. Every shred of our privacy is being ripped apart. As it is, we have an exaggerated sense of responsibility for not having been able to prevent the death of our loved ones. Please don't make it harder for us. Instead, show unconditional positive regard. Say 'You did your best', 'You were a great support', 'It is not your fault'. Such words are salve for the soul.

Don't make statements such as 'Suicide is an act of cowardice' or 'Suicide is the result of selfishness'. They are inaccurate and hurtful. Such value judgements criminalise our loved ones. In life, they were loving and responsible husbands, wives, daughters, sons, uncles, aunts, friends and grandparents, and they were also in tremendous psychological pain. Remember them fondly and for the way they lived their lives, not for the way they died. Suicide cannot define them. Your willingness to look at other aspects of our loved one's life will help us to do so too. Otherwise, we feel ashamed and we try to divorce them from our memory, which impairs our healing.

Don't give us unsolicited advice. We are capable of finding the answers we seek, at our own pace. Please don't assume responsibility for our lives. Instead, show that you truly care. Ensure that we get plenty of nourishment and sleep. Encourage us to take care of ourselves.

Don't condole with us just because it's the thing to do. And please don't use the condolence visit to gather juicy titbits about our loved one's death to enliven your conversations. Don't just say a few superficial words, or worse, make silent accusations, and then disappear.

Be proactive. We would like you to accompany us on our journey through suicide grief. This is a lifelong journey, and you can help us navigate the road ahead. Please read about suicide grief and how you can help. Birthdays, wedding anniversaries, death anniversaries and festivals are painful reminders of our loved one's absence. While you cannot take their place, you can certainly make our loss more bearable in many ways. For example, you can include us in get-togethers or call to find out how we are.

Simply listen. Through evocative body language, let us know that you are there for us. This sends out a 'no pressure' invitation to talk, if we feel like it. We need that reassurance because telling our stories over and over is one of the ways in which we heal.

Talk to mental health professionals and other people with lived experience of suicide loss to understand the complexity of the issue. Suicide grief is isolating and alienating. You can be a bridge of hope and connection.

Mind Your Language, Please

> One might argue that there is nothing really alarming about the words themselves [such as 'committed suicide'], and that they are standard descriptions of a tragic act. This was certainly true for me before I was attuned to the finer nuances and deeper connotations of these descriptions.
> —Robert Olson, *Suicide and Language*

One might argue that there is nothing alarming about phrases like 'committed suicide' and that they are standard descriptions of a tragic act. This was certainly true for me before I became attuned to the finer nuances and deeper connotations of such descriptions. However, if we need to change the perception of and the conversation around suicide, it is important to recognise that most of the words we hear in association with it are grossly insensitive and therefore need suitable alternatives.

- 'commit suicide'
- 'suicide victim'
- 'suicide attempter'
- 'successful suicide'
- 'completed suicide'
- 'failed suicide attempt'
- 'political suicide'
- 'suicide epidemic'

When you come across these phrases, do you find them insensitive? Do you ever pause and wonder how it could impact those who have lost a loved one to suicide or those who have tried to end their lives? Or do they seem acceptable and familiar to you? Chances are that unless you have been impacted in some way by suicide, you will wonder, what's in a word? Well, a lot.

In my time as a suicide prevention activist, the insensitivity of people to suicide and suicide-related issues has never ceased to appal me. I was once invited to speak at a Women's Day function sponsored by a well-known radio station. At the end of my talk, the radio jockey commended me for being an inspiration, particularly to women. Especially since, as he put it, my husband had 'committed suicide'.

This incident highlights several problematic issues regarding the portrayal of suicide in public discourse. First, the RJ had no business revealing my status as a survivor of suicide loss without my consent. It was particularly insensitive because I had chosen not to reveal it in my conversation with him—I didn't think it was relevant. By making an out-of-context reference to suicide, he sensationalised it. Secondly, the use of the phrase 'committed suicide' placed the act in the context of criminality and illegality, which only perpetuate the stigma attached to it. While his intention may not have been malicious, his impact on me was violative and intrusive.

I must admit that until I was personally affected by suicide loss, I too was unaware of the ways in which language perpetuates and reinforces negative stereotypes. As a communications professional in the disability and LGBTQIA+ spaces, I am familiar with the use of people-first language, which puts people before their disease or disability. For example, instead of saying a 'mentally ill person', we speak of a 'person with mental illness' as a way of acknowledging that mental illness is simply one facet of the person's life and not their entire identity.

If it is true that language is power, then words are not as innocuous as they seem. Embedded in every word is a range of connotations or associations. These influence, shape and define societal attitudes toward any issue, particularly those to do with mental illness, suicide, HIV/AIDS, and gender identity and sexual orientation, all of which tend to be perceived within the framework of morality.

Two years ago, when I read Canadian author and librarian Robert Olson's remark that the usage of 'commit suicide' is so common that one could be excused if one thought the word was hyphenated, it was an 'aha' moment for me. While my background in social sciences communications had attuned me cognitively to sensitive and appropriate use of language, my new reality as a survivor of suicide loss helped me make the switch instantly. That was the moment I stopped saying 'committed suicide'. And I didn't stop there. Every time I hear somebody use that phrase—and this includes most mental health professionals—I politely but firmly request them to stop using it and replace it with other sensitive phrases like 'death by suicide' or 'died by suicide'. I am prepared to engage in a conversation with them in case they are curious, which most of them are. Have I brought about a social transformation? No. Not yet. We all know that there is no magical way to achieve attitudinal transformation. But I am trying because I refuse to be part of the stigma, shame, secrecy and silence around suicide.

Doris Sommer Rotenberg is a suicide prevention activist with lived experience of suicide loss. Having lost her son Arthur, an accomplished physician, to suicide, she established the Arthur Sommer Rotenberg Chair in Suicide Studies at the University of Toronto. She speaks forcefully about the need to decouple the language of suicide from morality and sin:

'"Commit suicide". Two words facilely used to describe the act of self-killing. I had never questioned the use of this phrase until my son took his life. We might begin by considering the words we use to describe this destructive act—particularly the phrase "commit suicide"—the expression "to commit suicide" is morally imprecise. Its connotation of illegality and dishonor intensifies the stigma attached to the one who died as to those who have been traumatized by this loss. It does nothing to convey the fact that suicide is [often] the tragic outcome of depressive illness and this, like any other affliction of the body or mind, has in itself no moral weight. Suicide has been demonized as a metaphor for moral weakness and failure. Many people consider any form of psychological vulnerability, including depression, as a moral lapse. We, therefore, need a new vocabulary based on safe messaging principles to create supportive spaces for compassionate conversations on suicide. We need stigma-reducing, people-first language to replace the stigma, shame, secrecy and silence around suicide.'

I find this a promising entry point for candid conversations on suicide. For most people, the idea that a convergence of multiple factors, not just one 'reason', leads to suicide is radical because it flouts conventional stereotypes. Nevertheless, it is important to provide people with context, an understanding of the many factors that lead to suicide, and give them a chance to mull over its complexity.

The fact is that effective suicide prevention efforts require a convergence of various stakeholders—healthcare providers, law enforcement, traditional and social media, government, private sector, research organisations, social agencies, religious leaders, families, people with lived experience, and communities.

The media, with its enormous reach and influence in shaping and influencing public opinion and initiating attitudinal shifts, has a huge role to play in this matter. Yet, when SPEAK invited media professionals in the city for a programme on responsible reporting of suicide in the media, only two people turned up.

But I persist. We need to keep chipping away at the looming mountain of stigma, even if just a tiny bit at a time. We need to keep tilling the field, sowing the seeds of attitudinal change, watering and fertilising the field—one step at a time.

'The language we use to describe suicide not only reflects our own attitude but influences those attitudes as well as the attitudes of others. A change in the words we use will not immediately dispel deep seated prejudices, but it will inhibit their expression and in doing so, prepare the ground for attitudinal change,' writes Doris Sommer Rotenberg.

Here, then, are a set of non-negotiable guidelines for responsible and sensitive reporting of suicide in the media.

Focus on accurate and responsible reporting. Reporting on suicide because it is newsworthy—thereby sensationalising, normalising and glorifying it—or presenting it as a solution to problems only perpetuates myths and misconceptions.

Take the opportunity to educate the public. Suicide is the result of a convergence of multiple factors: biological, psychological, social and environmental. However, most media reports focus on one single factor—academic failure or difficult interpersonal relationships, for example—as the sole cause for suicide when, in reality, it (sometimes) ends up being only a trigger.

Describe suicide trends accurately and without sounding an alarm. Use denotative language, not hyperbole. For example, you can say suicide is rising, but saying it is 'skyrocketing' is alarmist.

Avoid language that sensationalises or normalises. Suicide is neither a crime nor a sin; nor is it an act of cowardice or heroism. Suicide victims and survivors of suicide attempts are not heroes, zeroes or cowards, so do not label them as such.

Avoid using the word 'suicide' in headlines or placing the story on the front page. Sensationalism might trigger vulnerable people to attempt suicide, especially when it is a celebrity who has died thus. Use neutral headlines that don't trigger at-risk populations. While including certain information might be necessary, sensitivity and responsibility are important. If you feel compelled to note some relevant detail, report it lower down in the story and avoid placing it prominently.

Avoid insensitive use of language. Language mirrors thoughts and, in turn, reflects societal attitudes. Avoid using phrases such as 'committed suicide', 'suicide epidemic' or 'political suicide'. These only reinforce negative stereotypes. Whereas, sensitive and informed usage is an antidote to such negativity. For example, instead of 'suicide epidemic', use 'increasing rates of suicide'.

Avoid explicit descriptions of the method of suicide. These violate the dignity and privacy of the deceased and their families. They are also potential triggers for people with suicidal ideation.

Avoid using pictures or videos of the deceased and their families and publishing suicide notes. Survivors of suicide loss are traumatised by the incident. Pictures and videos violate their privacy. The dignity of the deceased is equally important. If required, use a picture of the person from earlier times.

Provide information on where to seek help. Include a comprehensive list of resources. Such information sends out a strong message that suicide is preventable. Include information that is relevant for suicide attempt survivors to enable them to seek appropriate psychosocial intervention and support, and for survivors of suicide loss to rebuild their lives after the tragedy.

Show consideration for survivors of suicide loss. Refrain from asking for interviews, sound bites and photographs in the immediate aftermath of the tragedy. The survivor's pain and dignity are non-negotiable. Newsworthiness is not.

Instead, talk about larger issues surrounding suicide. This is a tremendous opportunity to raise awareness about the public health aspect of suicide. Include relevant statistics, quote experts in suicidology and mental health, and include information about the warning signs of suicide and how one can help in prevention.

Anchor stories in optimism and hope. Include testimonials from experts about how suicide can be prevented with timely intervention. Also include testimonials from suicide attempt survivors and survivors of suicide loss who have rebuilt their lives with appropriate intervention and have moved through the tragedy to find meaning and purpose in their lives.

And last, but certainly not least, please don't judge or label what most of us cannot even begin to understand unless we have had the lived experience.

The Elusive New Normal

> The reality is that you will grieve forever. You will not 'get over' the loss of a loved one; you will learn to live with it. You will heal and you will rebuild yourself around the loss you have suffered. You will be whole again but you will never be the same. Nor should you be the same nor would you want to.
>
> —Elisabeth Kübler-Ross

The process of relearning, of learning to re-live after loss, is non-linear. For me, it was one step forward and ten steps backwards. I wallowed sluggishly in a giant vat of memories, dreams and desires. I struggled to live meaningfully and purposefully in the light of my loss, its shadow and the sadness. I am no longer the same person. The old me died along with Murali. However, out of the ashes of my sorrow and despair, a new me is emerging, slowly but surely. I now see a stranger in the mirror. Hopefully, I will befriend her one day.

Relearning the world is not easy. So much that I had taken for granted, for most part of my life, was suddenly out of reach. It was not simply about taking note of Murali's absence and deciding to move on. Our home was a landmine of memories. Every nook and crevice, every corner in the house reminded me of him. He was nowhere, and yet he was everywhere. Memory played a tantalising game of hide and seek with me.

'Finding our way in the world after bereavement, that is, relearning the world, is an organic process; a holistic process. It is not a matter of *learning information about the world*, but *learning how to be and act* in *the world* differently in the light of our loss,' writes Thomas Attig in *How We Grieve*.

Change is the only certainty in life. This is most evident in times of loss. The resulting change and transition force us to confront the illusion of permanence. Yet, consciously and unconsciously, we resist and cling tenaciously to the past. Perhaps the only ones who don't resist change are babies. I now had to create a new way of living without Murali—a way of living in which he would no longer be a physical presence but an ineffable memory, a tormenting presence in absence.

Many centuries ago, the ancient Greek philosopher Socrates made an observation about adapting to change. He said, 'The secret of change is to focus all your energy not on fighting the old but on building the new.'

In loss and transition discourse, the term 'new normal' is used to describe a new way of being and living that has become the standard or the norm after a drastic change in the life of the person. As I stood at the most challenging crossroads in my life, it seemed to me that everything had come down to two phases: before and after the suicide.

After all, we are woven with the warp and weft of our relationships, especially the one with our significant other. In my case, the yarn had knotted and dyed itself in the colours of grief. Although I tried to untangle the skein, I could no longer mend or reweave the tapestry of my life with yarn that had outlived its purpose.

The first year was the most challenging. The void threatened to engulf me. I tottered on the edge of the abyss, then plunged into an ocean of grief. It was a free fall; a deep dive into the turbulent depths of my psyche. Through cycles of self-reflection and looking inwards, I realised that I had to face, befriend and finally embrace my pain and sorrow.

Intuitively, I chose to brave the eye of the storm because turbulence is where growth is. During this process, I learnt to gradually develop a relationship with uncertainty, with the unfamiliar and the unknown. I was an explorer of the psyche on a lonely voyage. However, I realised very soon that I was not alone. My inner self offered me all the reserves and resources I needed. But first, I had to connect with this inner being, to ask and be prepared to receive help. The act of unconditional surrender to grief, rather than fighting, controlling or taming it, helped me stay afloat. We cannot control the wind or the tides; we can only yield and align ourselves with their elemental energy and be carried forward. As every surfer knows, you can't stop the wave; you learn to ride it, taking up the challenge one wave at a time.

I recognised that this would require tremendous courage. It seemed safer to stay within the tested waters of the comfortable and familiar. The easier default response was to use the crutches of busyness and work to deal with the grief. At the time, it was easy to throw myself into work and seek distraction from the pain.

Shortly after Murali's death, I held down a full-time job about which I was passionate. It involved considerable travel and interacting with diverse people. For several months, I lived out of a suitcase. While that seemed a viable short-term strategy, it only anesthetised me to the pain. I was dealing with my grief by substituting it with something else, not by facing it. My intuition told me that it would be wise to take a semi-sabbatical for a short time.

It was the best decision I could have made. Facing psychic turbulence head-on is an act of courage and faith. I was fearful and, often, the fear felt justified. Only by facing it, by being alive to the raw, naked splendour of my pain, and by paring it could I receive its hidden messages. Whenever a powerful wave of grief overwhelmed me, I surrendered to it. Initially, I floundered and was tossed about like driftwood on the ocean. Gradually, however, I learnt to relate to the turbulence with love and respect. The wave has no existence apart from the ocean, and Existence was inviting me to be part of, and experience, the Oneness.

One of the best-kept secrets of bereavement is that life doesn't go back to what it was; it doesn't get better, it only gets different. Audrey Stringer in *Scaling the Mountain of Grief: Creating a New Normal through Loss and Healing* talks about the 5As required to establish a new normal: acknowledge (the loss), acclimatise (give yourself time to adapt to the loss), assimilate (blend the loss into your life, but let it not define or restrict you), accept (loss is loss, things will never be the same again; they will be different) and affirm (you have all the reserves and resources you need to rebuild your life).

I was engaged in a constant tug-of-war between the past and the present. The past had a way of sneaking up at the most unexpected times and places. Seemingly innocuous triggers, such as the sound of Murali's favourite music, the sight of a fruit or the aroma of cooking could trigger a tidal wave of tears.

Murali used to enjoy my cooking. After the tragedy, every time I stepped into the kitchen, I'd break down. The new normal then was to disengage myself from cooking. Today, I cook sporadically, and it feels different. I am also no longer able to sleep in the bedroom we shared. I shifted upstairs and renovated the house. I bought new furniture and moved things around. Metaphorically, I was rearranging the pieces of my life.

The first year was that of 'magical thinking', as writer Joan Didion describes it in *The Year of Magical Thinking*. I yearned for Murali. I felt him walk out from the bedroom when I was working in the living room. I felt him at the dining table, asking for coffee. I longed for the safety and security of his presence. No matter how hard I tried, it was impossible to abdicate memory and nostalgia. I was a hostage to the tyranny of the past.

There was, in addition, considerable paperwork to be done. There were also the monthly mourning rituals—markers of transition that culminated in the first anniversary.

During the second year, I felt Murali's absence acutely. There was no going back. Magical thinking, in retrospect, has an adaptive function. But it had outlived its purpose. While the grief ambushes were no longer frequent, they still lurked nearby with predatory guile. They also showed up in a new version—grief bursts. As the name implies, these are short, sudden, high-intensity grief episodes in capsules. The grief seemed demonic—and I had to find a way to exorcise it.

The second year was when I truly began to befriend and embrace grief. I realised that it was an invitation to a deeper exploration. I also learnt to honour and acknowledge my willingness to engage with grief. It was a distinct shift in perspective: I began to perceive grief as nourishing and affirmative rather than destructive or harmful.

The journey of healing through grief can be paradoxical. On the one hand, I wanted to engage with it, and on the other, I wanted to control it. But I also began to be self-compassionate and celebrate my engagement with grief. In the early stages, it is natural to want to avoid grief. In fact, that is the emergency response, to cauterise the haemorrhage. Once the bleeding is controlled, though, there follows the need to re-engage.

Alan Wolfelt in *Living in the Shadow of the Ghosts of Grief: Step into the Light* talks about 'dosing', or the need to slice pain into manageable doses. 'The concept of dosing our grief recognizes that we cannot embrace the pain of grief all at once out of some ill-founded need to "overcome". Instead, we must allow ourselves to "dose" the pain—feel it in small waves; then allow it to retreat until we are ready for the next wave.'

The experience of pain, sorrow and suffering has the ability to transform us. Such is the alchemy of grief. For that to happen, I had to look at my grief through the lens of compassion, concern and care. I saw her as the Divine Mother, the devi I had exiled from my being. I had to invoke her carefully, listen to her and integrate her into my life. The journey has taken me three years, and I now co-exist amicably with her. She is a large part of who I am today, but she does not restrict me in any way. She pervades me, yet she does not loom over me. This has enabled me to fully integrate all aspects of both Murali and me into a new self. The Divine Mother's infinite wisdom and love nourish and nurture me. Her strength and resilience empower me.

In my healing, light and shadow, hope and despair, joy and sadness are harmoniously blended.

A year ago, I asked my uncle C.R. Kannan, 'Will I ever reach the shore?' I could see no horizon, no land mass, no respite.

'One day you will. Trust me,' he said.

And I did.

During my journey, I've often lingered in the past and trespassed into the future. But today, I am anchored on the seashore of a new reality. The ocean has rebirthed me, and like a conch, I carry the music of the ocean within me. The ocean is no longer turbulent. It has a placid, all-pervasive presence in my life. And there are new scalloped shorelines waiting to be explored.

Transforming through Trauma

> My barn having burned down, I can now see the moon.
> —Mizuta Masahide

Kintsugi is the ancient Japanese art of fixing broken pottery with powdered gold. Once completed, dazzling streaks of gold glint in the conspicuous cracks and each 'repaired' piece acquires a new identity. This art form celebrates each artefact's unique history by proudly displaying its fractures instead of hiding them, and highlights the ineffable beauty that exists in vulnerability and fragility.

For as long as I knew him, Murali never threw away any broken objects. He was an expert surgeon; he would 'fix' the broken pieces. A few months prior to his death, Malli, our Golden Retriever, had partially chewed up one of my books. Murali plastered the spine with adhesive tape. The book is now a treasure. After a loved one's death, even the mundane becomes sacred.

'When adversity strikes, people often feel at least some part of them—their views of the world, their sense of themselves, their relationships—have been smashed. Those who try to put back their lives together exactly as they were, remain fractured and vulnerable. But those who accept the breakage and build themselves anew become more resilient and open to new ways of living … Focussing on, understanding and deliberately taking control of what we do in our thoughts and actions can enable us to move forward in adversity,' writes psychologist Stephen Joseph in *What Doesn't Kill Us: The New Science of Posttraumatic Growth.*

It has been three years since I was left behind and two years since I began writing this book. These years have given me a certain perspective tempered with wisdom that has helped me heal and transform through my loss.

The fissures and fractures, the scars and scabs, the fault lines and crevices are all part of me. The human spirit is magnificent in its resiliency and its ability to heal the deepest wounds. The cracks and crevices remind me that I may be broken, but the spirit can never be crushed. The damage that life has inflicted on me has, in some ways, made me stronger, resilient, powerful, authentic, real. The wounds of the past have enabled and emboldened me to face the present. After all, a diamond is only a piece of charcoal that has withstood pressure exceptionally well and transformed into a thing of beauty.

People like me are individuals with a lived experience of suicide loss. However, the direct experience of suicide is not limited to loss survivors. There are also suicide attempters and those with suicidal ideation. Until recently, their voices were marginalised in suicide prevention discourse and interventions. The enormous personal and collective shame, and the culture of stigma around suicide also silences voices of dissent. However, people with lived experience of suicide, particularly those impacted by suicide loss, can be powerful change agents in suicide prevention. As a result of our first-hand experience of the tangible and intangible aspects of a suicide death, we can serve as catalysts for addressing the silence around this serious public health issue.

I firmly believe that formidable challenges require authentic responses. While creating awareness about suicide prevention, I always reference it with my own lived experience as a suicide loss survivor. I've noticed that this creates an instant connect with the audience. The most hardened cynic sits up in anticipation. Those impacted by a similar loss glimpse hope, however nebulous. A lived experience perspective preserves the dignity of the deceased and those impacted by the loss; it fosters trust. The openness on offer counters built-in resistance and opens doorways. It fosters a willingness to engage with the toxic silence, using the antidote of compassion.

In the end, our stories make us who we are. Our biographies become our destiny. People who die by suicide are not mere statistics or numbers. When loss survivors speak to be heard, people realise that here is someone for whom suicide is not a mere cognitive construct, but something based on direct first-hand experience. When I reveal my vulnerability, it evokes compassion in the audience. It also enables them to get in touch with the courage within themselves and to engage in a difficult conversation.

'We are experts by experience—people who have lived with mental health conditions, people who have been suicidal, people who are trauma survivors. That is just as valuable as the kind of academic credentials people earn. And it's incredible that we can work together as partners,' writes Leah Harris of the National Center for Trauma-Informed Care in Virginia, USA.

We are a bridge across troubled waters. When we move our experiences from the margin towards the centre, we can facilitate meaningful dialogues and empowering conversations with mental health professionals, people at risk, policymakers, media, law enforcement, the legal system and the society at large.

Most mental health narratives tend to equate trauma with pathology and PTSD. In the early stages of my grief, I was on tenterhooks because I anticipated the onset of full-blown PTSD. In fact, this idea has become so mainstream that PTSD has moved beyond a diagnostic label and become part of the psychobabble that we use so glibly. While it is certainly true that some persons who experience trauma develop PTSD, it is not the norm.

My transformative journey through trauma and my interactions with people impacted by different kinds of trauma helped me understand the need to foster empowering perspectives on trauma and resilience. The trauma of suicide loss is a huge part of who I am today, but it does not define or reduce me in any way. I have discovered my own resilience. Although much has been lost, much still remains.

Trauma narratives have long been the exclusive preserve of mental health professionals and academicians. Across the world, the prevalent medical and mental health discourse pathologises trauma. But the immediacy of lived experience endows survivors of suicide loss with the perspective to rewrite the narrative and move it away from a pathologised PTSD model towards a non-pathologised, empowering model. We need to acknowledge, validate and recognise the potential of traumatic events to facilitate growth and the healing that enables people to transform.

A responsible two-way dialogue on trauma and loss requires the involvement of people with lived experiences. The vibrant discipline of trauma care needs to widen its perimeters to include, integrate and elevate the expertise of people with lived experience as central to the narrative.

Currently, mainstream perspectives of trauma are synonymous with victimhood. The trauma narrative in healthcare, mental health and academia, and the voices of 'experts' hinge on this. It glosses over the question of agency or the autonomy of people impacted by trauma and instead segues into the PTSD narrative that is victimisation-centric.

Early in my bereavement, it was tempting to subscribe to the seductive 'I don't deserve this' mindset. Those around us also feed into and build that narrative. Victimhood is a default response to trauma that is an important part of our journey. However, it is a stage and not an identity. The challenge is to not get stuck there.

Despite being aware of its self-defeating and deceptive comfort, I often wallowed in victimhood. In the early stages, it was an essential pathway to healing. You can eventually enjoy the view from the mountains, but only if you have plumbed the valleys and gorges.

In the long run, victimhood fundamentally disempowers us because it robs us of our agency, our choices and options. Victimhood leaches resilience. It is difficult to exit its quicksand without honesty, self-awareness and support, for it implies powerlessness and hopelessness.

Life is about taking responsibility for ourselves and our choices. We cannot outsource it. In victimhood, however, we abdicate responsibility to other persons or circumstances. Therefore, responsibility becomes an act of courage, and our conscious, empowered responses in the aftermath of a trauma become milestones in our journey. While experiencing victimhood, we are also on the *dwara*, threshold, of survivorhood.

I consciously chose to move away from victimhood. Yet, I often slipped—as is only natural and to be expected. But when it happened, I handled it with self-compassion. Bringing it into the light of awareness allowed me to reclaim my power slowly and gently. I did not try to control, reject, resist or fight victimhood, or build a wall around it. Instead, I embraced it lovingly, with self-awareness. If I tried to push against it, it pushed back. It needed to be treated with immense respect and I had to hear what it was trying to communicate. I learnt not to demonise or glorify victimhood, since either of these polarities can be disempowering.

Viktor Frankl, psychiatrist and Holocaust survivor, is an icon of resilience and post-traumatic growth. In his path-breaking book *Man's Search for Meaning: The Classic Tribute to Hope from the Holocaust*, he writes, 'When we are no longer able to change a situation, we are challenged to change ourselves. In some ways suffering ceases to be suffering at the moment it finds a meaning, such as the meaning of a sacrifice.'

In the 1990s, psychologists Richard Tedeschi and Lawrence Calhoun coined the term post traumatic growth (PTG) to describe the dramatic growth and transformation that some individuals experience after incredibly challenging life events. The idea that adversity can be an engine that drives growth seems radical. After all, there are more positive and pleasant ways of growing that are not painful. However, for PTG to occur, the adversity must have been of a seismic magnitude. In other words, it must have shattered your assumptions about life, highlighted the uncertainty and unpredictability of life, and revealed your vulnerability.

I was a witness to all this. At a forked path, I had two choices: to sink (victimhood) or swim and reach the shore (survive and thrive). I rejected victimhood and moved beyond to survive and thrive. Doing so not only enabled me to get back on track but also to move forward and progress—a key aspect of PTG.

Do we rebuild or do we sit in the rubble? When we rebuild, it is not from the rubble of the past. Clearing the debris is a part of the process. Holding on to it only slows us in our journey. The new normal after a tragedy is a rebirthing. I didn't strive to recreate the old life. That was gone forever. It had to be a new way of life that honoured and respected the past but moved forward authentically through the loss.

When I say I took responsibility for my life, I do not mean I took responsibility for Murali's decision to end his life. Or for the incident. I did not demonise or glorify the incident and the person. My life is now, and hereafter, about me. For most of my life, I had been living other people's versions of what my life should be. I wanted to reclaim my power and rescript my life. Slowly but surely, I began to move away from the incident, the circumstances and even the experience. As the new me emerged, the old, the outdated and the inauthentic gradually fell away, like a snake shedding its old skin to revel in the new.

Three years after Murali's death, the pain still lingers, but I have embraced growth. I find comfort in the fact that he and I shared a deep karmic bond. In the Vedantic tradition, this is referred to as *runanubandha*—the karmic hooks that fetter two people. Murali helped me learn what was required for me to move on in my karmic path. Our journey together was a karmic adventure. Together, we scaled the highest peaks and touched bottomless depths. I am wistful about the might-have-beens in our life together. I will forever cherish him; his passion, purpose and poise continue to inspire me. His quest for excellence is a legacy I cherish. I would like him to be remembered for the purposeful way he lived his life and his *svadharma* as a gifted doctor, not for how he died.

Emptying myself of the old and making it an offering at the shrine of nostalgia is an ongoing *sadhana*, spiritual pursuit. I have looked sufficiently long at the rear-view mirror. It is now time to keep my eyes on the road ahead, although I will occasionally, cautiously, look into the rear-view mirror whenever necessary. The new normal, for me, is about accommodating and assimilating the pain into my life. The alchemy of grief is about transmuting pain and sorrow into a dazzling version of myself—an iridescent plumage of the *nava rasa*, the nine emotions—love (*sringara*), laughter (*hasya*), compassion (*karuna*), anger (*raudra*), courage (*virya*), wonder (*adhbhuta*), fear (*bhayanaka*), disgust (*bhibatsa*) and peace (*shantam*). And I continue to be amazed by the human capacity for growth and transformation through loss.

Radical Self-care for Survivors

> To practice extreme self-care you must learn to love yourself unconditionally, accept your imperfections and embrace your vulnerabilities.
> —Cheryl Richardson, *The Art of Extreme Self-care*

The very idea of survivors of suicide loss practising self-care can seem radical. The stigma faced by a survivor invisibilises, erases and marginalises all of their valid concerns. Equally, most survivors themselves feel they are not entitled to any form of support, either from themselves or from others.

Cheryl Richardson's *The Art of Extreme Self-care* was a milestone in my path toward healing. 'Extreme self-care meant taking my care to a whole new level—a level that seemed arrogant and selfish, practised by people who had an inappropriate sense of entitlement. It meant taking radical action to improve my life and engaging in daily habits that allowed me to maintain this new standard of living. The practice of extreme self-care forces us to make choices and decisions that honor and reflect the true nature of our soul.'

On a fundamental level, self-care for survivors of suicide loss is about extraordinary self-compassion. It is about making the conscious choice to love ourselves unconditionally, accepting our imperfections and embracing our vulnerabilities. Our world has been ripped apart by a tragedy that has left deep craters and gaping wounds in our psyche. We need to establish a new normal that not only honours and respects the loved one whom we lost but also enables us to rescript our lives as we move forward through the tragedy.

Each survivor of suicide loss grieves differently. There are no Band-Aids, quick fixes or a one-size-fits-all approach to healing. That said, here are a few tips for radical self-care that helped me heal and transform:

First things first. Attend to your basic needs. Ensure that you eat nourishing food, drink plenty of water and have adequate rest and sleep. In the acute phase of traumatic grief, survivors may experience a loss of appetite. Or they may be tempted to binge and overeat. It is quite likely that you will find a good night's sleep elusive. Intrusive memories, crying spells and sheer exhaustion can prevent you from falling asleep or wake you up after a short spell of exhausted sleep. I found it helpful to take prescription sleep medicines in the first month following the tragedy. Then, as I built my resources, I gradually tapered off the dosage under medical supervision.

Stay with your feelings. In the acute phase of bereavement (the first three months, for me), I was overwhelmed by emotions like anger, sadness, rejection, abandonment and fear. It may be tempting to accept the well-meaning advice from friends and family to 'fight, conquer or subdue' your difficult emotions. But I found (and still find) these militaristic metaphors to be disempowering, self-defeating and non-sustainable. Instead, I would say, stay with your feelings and face them. It requires courage to do this because they often ambush you with the ferocity of a predator. But it is important to validate every feeling. Avoid labelling or judging them.

Treat yourself with utmost compassion. You owe it to yourself. We are so conditioned to expect love from the outside. Instead, we need to give it to ourselves. Be gentle with yourself.

'When you treat and view yourself with the respect you deserve, you experience the peace that comes from being present to yourself (…) it forces the ego to step aside as you experience a moment of seeing your true nature: a spiritual being housed in a physical shell,' says Richardson in her book.

Express yourself. Give yourself permission to acknowledge, explore, express and honour every emotion. I found journaling and adult colouring books particularly helpful.

Seek out support groups. Listening to other people's experiences of loss, how they responded, the challenges they faced and their strategies serve to normalise the experience of suicide loss and make us feel that it can happen to anyone at any time. We come to realise that we, the survivors of the loss, are in no way responsible for our loved one's act.

Seek out counselling services and therapies that are trauma-informed and loss-centric. I explored several body-based therapeutic modalities such as gestalt therapy, IEMT, core transformation and psychodrama (both in groups and individual settings) that helped me pare away the different layers of grief. I found that most mental health professionals had inadequate knowledge about counselling survivors of suicide loss. I responded to this lacuna by qualifying myself as a life coach who specialises in loss and transition.

Make changes in your physical environment. I made the difficult choice to continue to live in the same place where I had lost my loved one. Despite the trauma, the home which my late husband and I had lovingly built held happy memories for me. Besides, I could not deal with another transition at that point in my life. Since I had chosen to continue living there, I decided to make several changes in the physical space. Repainting the house, rearranging the furniture, getting rid of junk, decluttering and buying a few new artefacts gave the house a new look. It became symbolic of my effort to rearrange my life.

Surround yourself with supportive family and friends. Besides my birth family, I had (and still have) friends who were unconditionally loving and supportive. Soon after the tragedy, my elderly parents decided to divide their time between Chennai (where they live) and Madurai. They have been the central pillars in my healing. My closest friends in Madurai opened their doors to me. In the early stages of grief, it was impossible for me to stay at home in the late evenings as memories would assault me. I would go over to their homes, spend time with them, have dinner and then head back. It made all the difference. They would phone me every day to enquire how I was doing, and it helped to know that they cared about how I was coping.

Explore traditional systems of healing. In the early stages of grief, I had intractable headaches and elevated blood pressure. I was unable to process my thoughts clearly because of brain fog. The latter lifted in a couple of months, but the headaches didn't stop and the medications I took for it didn't help. In desperation, I tried acupuncture, Bach flower remedy, ayurveda and marma massage therapy. The headaches miraculously disappeared. Since then, I have been regularly following all four modes of treatment. They worked for me at the physical, emotional and spiritual levels and helped me process the grief organically and viscerally. Grief is not something that only exists in the mind, it is stored in every cell in the body. Deep tissue massage and massage techniques along the nerve meridians gradually restored my vitality and wellness in a holistic manner.

Develop new hobbies, find creative outlets. I acquired new hobbies—drawing and painting. I also re-engaged with travel and writing. Wildlife photography, tarot and oracle card reading, exploring energy-based healing techniques, getting involved in suicide prevention activism—pursuits like these helped me transform my pain into a purposeful energy.

Dealing with triggers. My wedding anniversary, the anniversary of my spouse's death and his birthday are powerful triggers that unleash a tsunami of memories. I deal with them by visiting my parents or going to the Sri Krishna temple in Guruvayoor, my *ishta devata*, cherished deity. I experienced several miraculous experiences at this sacred spot that helped me heal.

Empower yourself with knowledge. I read extensively about suicide and survivors of suicide loss. The resources and other material that I found both online and in books enabled me to acquire informed perspectives that have empowered me.

Anchor yourself in spirituality. This has been the central pillar of my healing journey. I committed to my daily *sadhana* with renewed vigour. This included a *kriya*—a process known as the Eight Spiritual Breaths—along with praying, practising pranayama, yoga and meditation. For two years now, I have been reciting the *Sri Vishnu Sahasranamam* daily and spending time in Vedic chanting. The concept of *sharanagati*, aligning with a higher force, is now an integral part of my life and one that has helped me stay the course. I am also a student of Vedanta, and being anchored in the Vedantic tradition has enabled me to achieve a degree of equilibrium and poise that would not otherwise have been possible.

The Oyster and the Pearl

> All art is autobiographical. The pearl is the oyster's autobiography.
>
> —Federico Fellini

A month before the first anniversary of Murali's death, I visited the picturesque island of Dhanushkodi at the southernmost tip of India. I walked along the deserted beach, gazed at the placid ocean and felt the waves wash over my feet. A few fisherpeople were seated in their makeshift tents, weaving and mending their nets. Catamarans were hauled up on the seashore. Seagulls flew close to the water, hawking for prey and whipping up foam as their wings scraped the sea's surface. The salty, tangy wind tousled my hair and invited me to let go. There were new shores waiting to be discovered, but to discover them, I had to have the courage to lose sight of the older shorelines.

Out of nowhere, an elderly fisherman, with a wizened face weathered by the sun and the wind, walked towards me. I looked up, puzzled.

'This is for you,' he said.

An oyster shell lay cradled in his palms, glistening in the sun. Embedded in it were seven iridescent pearls.

'I found them this morning when I returned from the sea. I don't know why I want to give it to you.'

I received the gift in silence, with reverential wonder. According to Zen wisdom, 'When the student is ready, the teacher appears.' And this oyster taught me some incredible lessons.

The pearl is created in pain. When faced with an irritant, the oyster does not withdraw. Instead, it draws on its infinite resources to cover the irritant with layer upon layer of a healing mineral substance known as nacre. Over a period spanning several years, the oyster transforms a wound caused by purely accidental circumstances into pearls.

I caressed the contours of the shell as the fisherman watched me. Perhaps he was telling me that pearls are not found on the seashore. To find them, you have to dive deep into the ocean. I was reminded of Rumi's words, 'What strikes the oyster shell does not damage the pearl.'

In these past three years, I have dived deep into the ocean of grief and pain. The fisherman was right. I did not find the pearls right away. However, in the stillness of the ocean, I heard myself for the first time. My desires, hopes and aspirations, and the whispers of my *atma* were amplified in the silence around me. I resurfaced finally, clutching pearls of wisdom. In transforming my wounds into wisdom, I surrendered to the spirit of the ocean. Today, I hear the sibilant whispers of the waves and the echo of the oceanic wisdom in the pearls.

I spread before you the pearls from my underwater exploration, which helped me navigate the grieving process and learn to engage with life meaningfully.

Accept your loss. Your life has changed forever. The loss is irreversible. Your tears, longing, pity, piety—nothing can alter the outcome.

Stop asking, why me? There are no answers. Instead ask, why not? And ask, what next?

Take ownership of your life. You, and you alone, are responsible for your life. Whether you yield or transform, the choice is yours.

Pain is inevitable; suffering is optional. You had no control over the cause. But you can control the outcome by choosing how to respond.

Adversity is a matter of chance; the response to it is a matter of choice. You have no control over what happens to you. But you have full control over how you choose to respond.

Chances and choices can affect you, but cannot define or destroy you. Stand up for yourself. Nobody can, or should, do it for you. Refuse to be a victim.

Reclaim your power. Circumstances have no power over you. You are the author of your destiny.

Pick up the pieces after a fall. You have the power and the responsibility to rebuild your life.

Transmute wounds to wisdom. Bring your awareness to 'fixing' your life. Lovingly heal your wounds with the golden glue of wisdom. You owe it to yourself.

Be proud of your scars. Your scars are an important part of you.

Be like the resilient oyster. Discover the poetry of your being through pearls of grit and grace. Your wisdom is your pain transformed.

Be flexible. Flow like the water; bend like the reed. Life is waiting to flow through you. Be open to grace.

Grieving is a solitary journey. Your journey is yours and yours alone. Others may help you, walk with you, accompany you, but the journey, ultimately, is only yours. You will find your peace, but alone.

Be compassionate to yourself. Grieving is incredibly challenging. It is uphill all the way. It is okay to fall, slip or falter, but persist you must. Otherwise, how will you get to gaze at the panorama of life from the mountaintop?

Travel free and travel far. Give yourself permission to wander. Throw away your maps and the GPS. Tune into your intuition to discover new shorelines.

Trust the process of life. Life is uncertain and unpredictable. Surrendering to a higher power will ensure that you float and not sink. The ocean may be turbulent, but stay attuned to the force within. Nothing in life is accomplished through fear.

You will be whole again, but never the same. Grief changes you inside out. Acknowledge and celebrate the new you. For the new you to emerge, the old has to be destroyed, and the debris cleared.

Grief doesn't get better; it feels different. Grief will not go away or disappear someday. It decreases in intensity. It becomes easier. But it will linger forever.

Cherish your blessings. Gratitude keeps the blessings flowing into your life. Despite everything, it is a beautiful world.

Life is a matter of perspective. Whether you want the view from the mountaintop or the valley, you get to choose.

Cherish your loved one's legacy. Remember and honour your loved one for the way they lived their life, not for the manner of their death.

Ask for help. Let people know that you would like them to support you. Ask and you will receive. You cannot expect others to read your mind.

Cultivate a tribe or community. Supportive relationships buffer the impact of the loss and facilitate transition. We need accompaniment in grief, especially in the early stages.

Spring-clean and declutter your mind. Let go of the old and make room for the new. Unless you empty yourself, you cannot receive.

Choose your focus. Thoughts have energy. Whatever you focus your attention on will manifest itself. If you cling to the past, you stagnate. Be mindful of your thoughts and feelings. They will shape the quality of your life.

Live in the moment. Live like a trapeze artist. Know when to hold on and when to let go. Life is a balancing act.

Resilience is the norm, not the exception. Most people not only survive, they thrive, bouncing back and moving forward after every challenging experience. There is something extraordinary in the ordinary.

Every rose has a thorn. Joy and sorrow are free of personal biases. Everyone gets a mixed blessing. Some roses, however, have more thorns. Smell the roses and savour their fragrance anyway.

Be a pragmatic optimist. Know what you can change and have the courage to make those changes. Gain the wisdom to know the difference between what you can and cannot change.

Draw on your resources. All the resources that you need to navigate crises lie within you. Look within. Dive deep within yourself. You are certain to surface with pearls of wisdom.

Re-engage with the world, one step at a time. Learning to re-engage with the world is like running a marathon. Small, purposeful steps that allow you to sample life in small doses is the key. Neither fasting nor feasting helps. Moderation does.

Find meaning and purpose in life. Move through tragedy and still live a meaningful, joyous life. A loss is a semicolon in your life, not a full stop.

Embrace your grief. Give yourself permission to experience grief—the sadness, fear, anger, guilt, remorse. Embrace every emotion in the grief spectrum.

Paint the canvas of your life with the colours of the rainbow. Light is not the absence of colour but a blend of the seven colours of the rainbow—VIBGYOR (vulnerability, inventiveness, buoyancy, grace and grit, yielding oceanic resourcefulness).

Light up your life. Against the expanse of unbounded space, into the earthen lamp of authenticity, pour the oil of pain and sorrow, and use the wick of awareness to light up your life with the fire of wisdom and awareness. Dance joyously. Your joys are your sorrows transformed.

Churning the Ocean of Grief

> And once the storm is over, you won't remember how you made it through, how you managed to survive. You won't even be sure whether the storm is really over. But one thing is certain. When you come out of the storm, you won't be the same person who walked in. That's what this storm's all about.
>
> —Haruki Murakami, *Kafka on the Shore*

Dark clouds of sorrow had blotted out the light from my life. The total solar eclipse threatened to linger for eternity as I plunged headlong into the depths of grief. It was a *thirtha yatra*, a pilgrimage, a sacred journey into the depths of my being.

Like the *samudra manthana*, the churning of the ocean in the Hindu dharma tradition, my psyche was churned for hidden treasures. My loving family and close friends were the mountain Mandara, the bedrock of events. In place of the snake Vasuki, I used the braided rope of my determination and resilience. When grief storms threatened to cast away my family and friends, they were anchored by the divine, the *kurma* or tortoise that ensured stability in chaos. Holding the rope at either end, the forces of light and shadow within my psyche did the actual work of churning.

The ocean roiled, heaved and surged for three years. However, after some time, even though the churning continued, I discovered sacred spaces within my psyche that were impervious to the turbulence. In these spaces of stillness, I discovered pearls of wisdom, guided by *shantam* (quietitude), *karuna* (compassion) and *ramyam* (joyous wonder).

I tried using force to dislodge my grief, but it clung stubbornly, so I embraced it instead, in its raw, visceral, primal intensity. I let it bombard me with exquisite pain. The antidote for *shoka* (sorrow), I learnt, is journeying through the process, immersing in it, and emerging purified and healed. And *shoka* can be transformed to *sloka* (verse).

Touching the core of my sorrow, I witnessed my own inner turmoil with *vairagya* (a certain distance and dispassion). I sensed the pervasive presence of *karuna* (compassion)—for Murali and my family, for those who were no longer a part of my life and for myself. Blocks dissolved, barriers disappeared, and opposites merged as I touched eternity. *Ananda* (bliss) filled every pore of my being. My cells danced in delirious joy. I was ready for the ascent in a state of *gati* (flow). Through the sacred act of *prayaschitham* (reconnecting with my highest self), I healed the wounds in my psyche. I think I earned the right to *amrita*, the elixir of peace, wisdom, compassion and love.

I rose from the ocean like Sri Lakshmi—stronger and wiser, purified and healed. As I began moving forward, every moment reminded me that even monumental sorrows can be left behind, one step at a time.

Afterword

Practical and Pioneering

I am so honoured and privileged to be asked to write the afterword to Nandini Murali's magnificent and life-affirming book *Left Behind* about the suicide of her beloved husband, Dr T.R. Murali, the distinguished physician and surgeon who practised medicine in Madurai. Dr Murali was well-known and universally respected for his pioneering work in the field of urology.

I, too, lost my urologist husband Harry Reiss, a prominent New York City doctor, to suicide many years before and many continents away. Harry killed himself on 16 December 1989 at the age of forty-three. We were married for twenty-one years and, like Nandini, I had accompanied him on his long medical journey to become a physician who devoted his life and career to helping others. Yet, at the prime of his life and his career, Harry injected himself with a lethal dose of the anaesthetic thiopental. I found him dead in his office, after he was late in returning home and I could not reach him.

Suicide is not spoken about openly or easily—there is a wall of silence surrounding this mysterious topic, probably because the pain is so private and the act so public. But now, luckily, we have this profoundly insightful and helpful book for all survivors of suicide loss. I, who have never stopped looking for answers to the 'why' of Harry's suicide more than thirty years after his death, raced through these pages with nods of recognition and pauses of gratitude for having been given a deeper knowledge of the unique circumstances that lead to the suicide of a loved one. I also had the opportunity to get to know the significance of Dr Murali's life and the legacy he left behind.

In this finely crafted and compellingly readable book, Nandini sensitively and humanely communicates her own personal story as well as the stories of the families and loved ones of others who have died by suicide. Her writing is honest and real, strong and vulnerable, practical and professional, caring and compassionate. Nandini opens a window into what she describes as the 4S's of suicide: stigma, shame, secrecy and silence. She not only relates her own story of incalculable loss but also tells the stories of others, like myself, who continue to wrestle with the unique grieving and mourning that follow the suicide of a loved one.

All survivors of suicide loss will welcome Nandini's practical and pioneering advice about how to develop resilience while never forgetting the person we have loved and lost. I highly recommend this book to all survivors of suicide loss. By letting us into her life with her cherished husband, she grants us insights as well as new friends in our voyage to healing and strength.

'To discover new oceans, you must have the courage to lose sight of the shore,' Nandini writes. 'In loss and transition discourse, the term "new normal" is used to describe a new way of being and living that has become the standard or the norm after a drastic change that has transpired in the life of the person. Here I was, at the most challenging crossroads in my life, which now consisted of two phases: before and after the suicide.'

Thank you, Nandini, for this invaluable resource that is much needed, much welcomed and much appreciated. On behalf of all survivors of suicide loss and the memories of those left behind, I remain grateful for your courage, strength and guidance.

From one survivor to another,
Carla

Carla Fine is the author of No Time to Say Goodbye: Surviving the Suicide of a Loved One.

Science and Spirituality

On 27 April 2017, Dr Nandini Murali, a gender and diversity professional, lost her urologist husband Dr T.R. Murali to suicide. She writes: 'That was the day one death by suicide killed two. That was the day I lost my precious partner. That was the day the sun plunged into darkness. That was the day my life changed forever.'

And what this amazing woman has done since that day! With candour and soul-searching honesty, Dr Murali walks us through the early minutes, hours, days, weeks and months of her changed life. On the first anniversary of her husband's death, she created SPEAK, an initiative to change conversations on suicide and promote mental health. By talking openly about her husband's death and her tireless advocacy work, she is trashing the soul-destroying stigma that for too long has enshrouded those who die by suicide and those in its wake.

Left Behind is a slim memoir, beautifully written and gripping. It is laced with stories of other people, many of whom have lost family members to suicide—and their travails and insights. Dr Murali educates the reader with passages from some of the leading experts and researchers on suicide across the globe. Her mix of science with the power of religion and spirituality is refreshing and laudatory. Her sage advice is elemental and practical. Her empathy for her husband and others who have taken their lives is palpable, as in this sentence, about finding her husband lying on the bathroom floor: 'The sadness on his face will forever be engraved in my memory.'

This is a must-read for a wide audience: those bereaved by suicide, those individuals living with a mental illness, those health professionals who treat them, and those who care about a subject that touches us all.

Michael F. Myers

Michael F. Myers is a professor of Clinical Psychiatry, SUNY Downstate Health Sciences University, Brooklyn, New York, and author of Why Physicians Die by Suicide: Lessons Learned from Their Families and Others Who Cared.

Looking Truth Straight in the Eye

When I was first introduced to Dr Nandini Murali a couple of years ago, I was told that she was a writer who was keen to write on mental healthcare. Ever since, through several rounds of meetings and telephone calls, she has helped me understand the numerous layers of the complex subject of suicide and suicide loss.

One of the most remarkable layers of suicide is the identity that society delivers to those dear ones who are left to cope with the loss. 'A survivor of suicide loss', as an identity, is an unbearable burden they spend their lifetime coming to terms with.

Kudos to Nandini's boundless grit and unconditional empathy. She refused to live with the identity society wanted to give her. It was her guru's mantra that helped her become resilient and confront the many emotional, social and physical challenges she had to experience.

Making her own loss and grief the basis of her journey, she decided to serve those who struggle to cope with the loss of suicide. She knew very well that this path would require her to relive those difficult moments a million times. But, in our conversations, I saw the steely determination with which she had resolved to move ahead.

This soul-searching book is Nandini's gift to the world. This is not just a memoir but a message, that to be able to cope with such unspeakably difficult moments, we need to look truth straight in the eye. Her narrative honesty is a demonstration of her keen desire to help the many who are trying to find answers that continue to elude them.

As much as this book is for those who survived the loss, it is also for all those who have been touched by it, even in the remotest way. When we read a newspaper report of suicide and frame an opinion, and sometimes make unwarranted comments, we must know that we have automatically become a stakeholder of this landscape.

If the book inspires the former to build emotional resilience, it also asks us to deeply reflect upon our thoughts, views and actions around those who have died of suicide and those who are dealing with the loss.

As we read this book, we must look for ourselves in it. Among the many uncles, aunts, friends, cops, support staff and colleagues in her stories, we must be able to find ourselves. We owe to it those to whom we so conveniently hand over a new identity for the rest of their lives.

We cannot thank Nandini enough for deciding to live through the pain, once again, for all of us.

Manoj Chandran

Manoj Chandran is the founding CEO of White Swan Foundation for Mental Health.

Fired by Purpose

> Ring the bells that still can ring
> Forget your perfect offering
> There is a crack in everything
> That's how the light gets in
> —Leonard Cohen

Life is not black or white, and in the grey lies the fountainhead of wisdom. Nandini and Murali, two people who travelled together. Murali struggling to find his inner equilibrium and Nandini coping with the ups and downs of day-to-day life, striving to help Murali find his inner peace. Murali knew that Nandini had in her the strength to overcome grief and chart a new way forward. Murali went on to find eternal peace. How has life unfolded for both of them?

Very few people in the world are faced with such intense challenges. Of the few, a handful fight back and become the source of courage and inspiration for others who struggle with the same challenges. Nandini, in her own ways, has coped with the grief and has found a purpose in life: to bring about greater awareness on mental health issues.

In my interactions with her in the early days of grief, I could see a courageous warrior who was trying to make sense of it all, while aspiring to bring clarity to people who were going through similar life situations. Nandini has chosen not to be a victim but a victor. Watching her from a distance and hearing about the work she does is an inspiration for me and, I am sure, for most people.

Her talks and writing are all focused on helping the cause. Sharing her story with sincerity and openness through this book shows the conviction that Nandini has in sharing with others her life and her struggle, so that people can find their own solutions and directions.

This is the beginning of a journey, and Nandini is driven by a fire from deep within. I am sure the coming decades will be the most meaningful and purposeful in her life.

Go on, Nandini, chart your own path and leave a trail for others to follow! We are awed looking at you blazing on and are cheering you all the way!

Aravind Srinivasan

Aravind Srinivasan is the director of projects at Aravind Eye Care System.

Bibliography

A, Srinivasa Raghavan, translator. *Sri Vishnu Sahasranamam: with the Bhashya of Sri Parasara Bhattar*. Sri Visishtadvaita Pracharini Sabha, 1983.

Anderson, Susan. *The Journey from Abandonment to Healing*. Berkley Books, 2014.

Attig, Thomas. *How We Grieve: Relearning the World*. Oxford University Press, 2011.

Baugher, Bob, and Jack Jordon. *After Suicide Loss: Coping with Your Grief*. Caring People Press, 2016.

Bering, Jesse. *Very Human Ending: How Suicide Haunts Our Species*. Black Swan, 2019.

Blackie, Sharon. *If Women Rose Rooted: The Journey to Authenticity and Belonging*. September Publishing, 2019.

Bonanno, George A. *The Other Side of Sadness: What the New Science of Bereavement Tells Us about Life after Loss*. Basic Books, 2009.

Brown, Brené. *Rising Strong*. Vermillion London, 2017.

Burgess, Mary S. *Handbook of Hope: First Aid for Surviving the Suicide of a Loved One*. Sonbeam Press, 2000.

Cacciatore, Joanne. *Bearing the Unbearable: Love, Loss, and the Heartbreaking Path of Grief*. Wisdom Publications, 2017.

Cameron, Julia. *Right to Write: An Invitation and Initiation into the Writing Life*. Hay House UK Ltd, 2017.

Cameron, Julia. *The Artist's Way*. Macmillan Publishers, 1993.

Cameron, Julia. *The Sound of Paper: Inspiration and Practical Guidance for Starting the Creative Process*. Penguin, 2006.

Cameron, Julia. *Walking in This World: The Practical Art of Creativity*. J.P. Tarcher/Putnam, 2003.

Campbell, Joseph. *The Hero with a Thousand Faces*. New World Library, 2008.

Carlson, Trudy. *Suicide Survivor's Handbook: A Guide to the Bereaved and Those Who Wish to Help Them*. Benline Press, 2000.

Chodron, Pema. *Taking the Leap: Freeing Ourselves from Old Habits and Fears*. Shambhala Publications, Incorporated, 2019.

Csikszentmihalyi, Mihaly. *Flow: The Psychology of Optimal Experience*. Harper Row, 2009.

Desikachar, T. K. V. *The Heart of Yoga: Developing a Personal Practice*. Inner Traditions International, 1995.

Devine, Megan. *It's Ok That You're Not Ok: Meeting Grief and Loss in a Culture That Doesn't Understand*. Sounds True, Incorporated, 2017.

Didion, Joan. *The Year of Magical Thinking*. CNIB, 2006.

Dreamer, Oriah Mountain. *The Invitation*. HarperSanFranciso, 2006.

Dunne, Edward J., et al. *Suicide and Its Aftermath: Understanding and Counseling the Survivors*. W.W. Norton & Company, 1987.

Easton, Amber Lea. *Free Fall: A Memoir of a Family Surviving the Suicide of a Loved One and Reclaiming Life on Their Own Terms*. Mountain Moxie Pub., 2013.

Fell, Lynda Cheldelin, et al. *Surviving Loss by Suicide: 12 True Stories about Surviving the Aftermath of Losing a Loved One to Suicide*. AlyBlue Media, 2015.

Fine, Carla. *No Time to Say Goodbye: Surviving the Suicide of a Loved One*. Doubleday, 2000.

Ford, Debbie. *The Secret of the Shadow: The Power of Owning Your Own Story*. HarperCollins, 2002.

Ghose, Aurobindo. *The Yoga and Its Objects*. Aurobindo Ashram Publication Department, 1992.

Gibran, Kahlil. *The Prophet*. Fingerprint Publishers, 2020.

Goleman, Daniel. *Destructive Emotions: A Scientific Dialogue with the Dalai Lama*. Bloomsbury India, 2013.

Griffiths, Jay. *Wild: An Elemental Journey*. Penguin Books, 2008.

Grollman, Earl A. *Suicide: Prevention, Intervention, Postvention*. Beacon Press, 1988.

Haymans, Kim. *Life Goes On: Picking Up the Pieces after a Loved One's Suicide*. Balboa Press, 2014.

Hanh Nhat. *Silence: The Power of Quiet in a World Full of Noise.* HarperOne, 2016.

Hone, Lucy. *Resilient Grieving: Finding Strength and Embracing Life after a Loss That Changes Everything.* The Experiment, 2018.

Jamison, Kay R. *An Unquiet Mind: A Memoir of Moods and Madness.* Picador, 2015.

Jamison, Kay R. *Night Falls Fast: Understanding Suicide.* Picador, 2012.

Joseph, Stephen. *What Doesn't Kill Us: The New Psychology of Posttraumatic Growth.* Basic Books, 2012.

Judith, Anodea. *Eastern Body, Western Mind Psychology and the Chakra System as a Path to the Self.* Jaico Publishing House, 2004.

Kabat-Zinn, Jon. *Wherever You Go, There You Are: Mindfulness Meditation for Everyday Life.* Piatkus, 2016.

Kumar, Sameet M. *Grieving Mindfully: A Compassionate and Spiritual Guide to Coping with Loss.* New Harbinger Publications, 2005.

Kübler-Ross, Elisabeth, and David Kessler. *Life Lessons: How Our Mortality Can Teach Us about Life and Living.* Simon & Schuster, 2014.

Kübler-Ross, Elisabeth, and David Kessler. *On Grief and Grieving: Finding the Meaning of Grief through the Five Stages of Loss.* Scribner, 2012.

Lakoff, George, and Mark Johnson. *Metaphors We Live By.* University of Chicago Press, 2003.

Levine, Peter A. *Healing Trauma: A Pioneering Program for Restoring the Wisdom of Your Body.* Sounds True, 2012.

Levine, Peter A., and Ann Frederick. *Waking the Tiger: Healing Trauma: the Innate Capacity to Transform Overwhelming Experiences.* North Atlantic Books, 1997.

Lewis, C. S. *A Grief Observed.* CrossReach Publications, 2016.

Lipsky, Laura van Dernoot., and Connie Burk. *Trauma Stewardship: An Everyday Guide to Caring for Self while Caring for Others.* Accessible Publishing Systems, Pty, Ltd., 2010.

Lukas, Christopher, and Henry M. Seiden. *Silent Grief: Living in the Wake of Suicide.* Jessica Kingsley Publishers, 2007.

Mabry, Richard L. *Tender Scar: Life after the Death of a Spouse.* Kregel Pub., 2017.

Maris, Ronald W., et al. *Comprehensive Textbook of Suicidology*. Guilford Press, 2000.

Mortali, Micah. *Rewilding: Meditations, Practices, and Skills for Awakening in Nature*. Sounds True, 2019.

Myers, Michael F. *Why Physicians Die by Suicide*. Michael F Myers, 2017.

Myers, Michael F., and Carla Fine. *Touched by Suicide: Hope and Healing after Loss*. Gotham Books, 2006.

Neeld, Elizabeth Harper. *Seven Choices: Finding Daylight after Loss Shatters Your World*. Warner, 2006.

Noel, Brook, and Pamela D. Blair. *I Wasn't Ready to Say Goodbye: Surviving, Coping, and Healing after the Sudden Death of a Loved One*. Sourcebooks, 2018.

Oliver, Mary. *New and Selected Poems, Volume One*. Beacon Press, 1992.

Oriah. *The Call: Discovering Why You Are Here*. HarperSanFrancisco, 2006.

Patel, Meera Lee. *Start Where You Are: A Journal for Self-Exploration*. Penguin Books Ltd, 2016.

Prechtel, Martín. *Smell of Rain on Dust*. North Atlantic Books, 2015.

Reivich, Karen, and Andrew Shatte. *The Resilience Factor: 7 Keys to Finding Your Inner Strength and Overcoming Life's Hurdles*. Broadway Books, 2003.

Rendon, Jim. *Upside: The New Science of Post-Traumatic Growth*. Touchstone, 2016.

Richardson, Cheryl. *Art of Extreme Self-Care: Transform Your Life One Month at a Time*. Hay House UK Ltd, 2019.

Sachdeva, Santosh. *The Eight Spiritual Breaths: Breathing Exercises and Affirmations That Transform Your Life*. Yogi Impressions Books, 2010.

Sandberg, Sheryl. *Option B*. Random House UK, 2019.

Sanders, Catherine M. *Surviving Grief ... and Learning to Live Again*. Wiley, 2015.

Seligman, Martin E. P. *Flourish: A Visionary New Understanding of Happiness and Well-Being*. Atria, 2013.

Shneidman, Edwin S. *Autopsy of a Suicidal Mind*. Oxford University Press, 2004.

Srimad Bhagavata Mahapurana. Gita Press, 2019.

Swami, Om. *When All Is Not Well: Depression, Sadness and Healing—A Yogic Perspective*. Harper Element, 2016.

Thompson, Mary Reynolds. *Reclaiming the Wild Soul: How Earth's Landscapes Restore Us to Wholeness.* Wild Roots Press, 2019.

Tolle, Eckhart. *The Power of Now: A Guide to Spiritual Enlightenment.* Hachette Australia, 2018.

Turner, Toko-Pa. *Belonging: Remembering Ourselves Home.* RIDER, 2017.

Vachani, Radhika. *Just Breathe: The Most Powerful Tool for Personal Transformation and Happiness.* Westland Publications Ltd, 2017.

Vasudev, Sadhguru. *Death: An Inside Story.* Penguin Ananda, 2020.

Viegas, Belinda. *The Cry of the Kingfisher.* Goa 1556, 2011.

Weller, Francis. *The Wild Edge of Sorrow.* North Atlantic Books, U.S., 2015.

Wilber, Ken. *Grace and Grit.* Shambhala, 2000.

Wolfelt, Alan D. *The Wilderness of Suicide Grief: Finding Your Way.* Companion, 2010.

Wolfelt, Alan. *Healing a Spouse's Grieving Heart: 100 Practical Ideas after Your Husband or Wife Dies: Compassionate Advice and Simple Activities for Widows and Widowers.* Companion Press, 2003.

Wolfelt, Alan. *Living in the Shadow of the Ghosts of Grief: Step into the Light.* Companion Press, 2007.

Wolfelt, Alan. *Understanding Your Grief: Support Group Guide—Starting and Leading a Bereavement Support Group.* Companion Press, 2004.

Wolfelt, Alan. *Understanding Your Suicide Grief: Ten Essential Touchstones for Finding Hope and Healing Your Heart.* Companion Press, 2009.

Yackley, Sel Erder. *Never Regret the Pain: Loving and Losing a Bipolar Spouse.* Helm Pub., 2008.

Zolli, Andrew, and Ann Marie Healy. *Resilience.* Headline/Business Plus, 2012.

Heartfelt Gratitude

Loss is loss. My life is no longer what it was. Indeed, even I am not who I was at the time of the tragedy.

My journey through the solitary landscape of grief has not been guided by maps or manuals. However, a handful of people have guided me like lighthouses across the ocean of grief and helped me discover a new shore. They have restored my faith in the goodness of people and I am blessed to have them in my life.

Shri Guru Rohit Arya, my spiritual guru, for his wisdom, compassion and protection. His sage advice on avoiding the victim trap was the resplendent full moon that guided my fragile raft across the turbulence.

My maternal uncle, P.S. Ranganathan, the wisest elder I have known, whose constant reminder to bow down before *bhagavat sankalpam* (divine determination) anchored my journey in a Vedantic perspective.

My parents Sudha Raman and C.R. Raman, for demonstrating through thought, word and deed that it *is* possible to face any tragedy with grace, grit and grounded resilience. They inspire me to be the best version of myself.

My mother, again, for introducing me to the study of Vedanta.

My brother C.R. Venkatesh, his wife Bhuvaneshwari and son Anirudh for their infinite love and loving presence. They anchor me and are the lambent light in my life.

My uncle Dr C.R. Kannan, for inspiring this book with his poignant emails. I still cherish the note cards he handwrote to me on a sunny May afternoon in Las Vegas in 2018 as the book evolved. Thank you for driving me to the Grand Canyon, for being the first reader of this book, for your prompt and perceptive inputs, and for championing me.

My uncle C.R. Sreedhar and aunt Mythili Sreedhar, who have always been proud of me.

My cousin Sriram Sreedhar, for his unconditional acts of love and generosity in the early days of the tragedy.

The Ramasubramanians, for being family to me.

Dr C. Ramasubramanian, for voyaging with me on the sacred journey though grief and enabling me to see new horizons, glimpse magnificent rainbows, discover new shores and transform through tragedy.

Dr Vikhram Ramasubramanian, for his love, sensitivity and generosity in helping me transition. I will always cherish what he did for Murali on the day he died.

Rajkumari Ramasubramanian, for opening her heart and home for me.

Dr R. Selvi, for whom I am the 'poster girl' for resilience, for our joyful conversations.

Dr M. Selvi, for letting me know early on that I stood rooted even in the worst phase of the tragedy; that I could be bent, but never broken.

Dr T. Balan Nair, for guiding my family and me with wisdom and loving kindness throughout the journey.

The Fomra family—Vidya aunty, Mamta, Ravi, Porvi and Dhevesh—for being my second family in Madurai.

Mamta Fomra, for our shared sisterhood. Her love and generosity are like rain on a parched land.

Dr R. Subramony, for his magnificent support.

Dr A. Mohan, Dr Sharmila Mohan and Harshita Mohan, for helping me cherish memories of Murali and cheering me all the way.

Dr A.B. Chitra, for always being there for me and believing in me.

Carla Fine, for her empathy and inspiration. She showed me that it takes outrageous courage to face outrageous loss.

Kamal Sahai, for reminding me that while it is important to honour the past, it is equally important to move towards the future.

T. Dhananjayan and Ishwari, for choosing to stay behind with me. I cherish their love and loyalty.

Bob, for prophetically pointing out that this book lurked in my talk at the inauguration of SPEAK.

Mary and Fred Munson, my 'American parents', for the healing conversations at their lovely home in Ann Arbor, Michigan, USA.

Dr Antony Fernandez, for the power of possibilities.

Dr Maitrayee Mukhopadhyay and Dr Franz Wong, for the European spring and our profound conversations.

K. Anandh, Dr Mohan Raj, Krish Srikkanth and Magdalene Jeyarathinam, for precious insights on grief and grieving.

Vasantha Santhanakrishnan, Sudha, A. Revathi, T. Dhananjayan, Carla Fine, P. Krishnan, Dr Mohan Raj, Dr A. Raja and Dr Meenakshi Raja, for sharing their stories of suicide loss with candour and courage.

P. Veeralakshmi, whose healing and wisdom have helped me navigate the slippery terrain of grief.

Karpagam Rajagopal, my classmate in school, whose perceptive inputs fine-tuned the narrative.

Kate Keisel, for her sensitivity and warmth, and the gift of her sacred friendship.

Raghu Ananthanarayanan, Sashikala Ananth and Anita Balasubramanian, for introducing me to the profundity of yoga philosophy and psychology.

Sri Bhavani Kumaran and Shenba Raman, who support my work in suicide prevention with sensitivity and commitment.

Laxmi Arjun, the daughter of my heart, for her gentle presence in my life.

My sacred companions: Malli, gorgeous Golden Retriever, 24/7 therapist, companion and foot warmer, and Minnal, adorable Rajapalayam, for filling my life with doggie love and wisdom.

Karthika V.K. and the team at Westland, for their efforts in co-creating the final version of this book. A special thank you to Karthika, whose sensitivity and informed perspectives propelled her to publish the book and mainstream a 'difficult' conversation.

Gavin Morris, for a spectacular cover design that reflects the essence of my journey. Perhaps this is one book that can be judged by its cover!

Dr T.R. Murali, my late husband and my greatest teacher. We were karmically yoked. His poise, precision and purpose continue to inspire me. I yearn for him. Now and forever.

The divine, the stable and sacred presence in my life that has steered me to a new shore, grounded me and helped me rise stronger and rooted, as I grew in aspirational glory, offering myself like a wild flower to the Great Creator and Supreme Artist.

www.ingramcontent.com/pod-product-compliance
Lightning Source LLC
LaVergne TN
LVHW010322070526
838199LV00065B/5638